PRACTICAL LABOR RELATIONS

A Collection of Readings

Edited by

Paul E. Hoffner

Robert L. Gaylor

With

Kathleen A. Rohaly

UNIVERSITY PRESS OF AMERICA

LANHAM • NEW YORK • LONDON

University Press of America,® Inc.

4720 Boston Way
Lanham, MD 20706

3 Henrietta Street
London WC2E 8LU England

Printed in the United States of America

British Cataloging in Publication Information Available

Library of Congress Cataloging in Publication Data

Main entry under title:

Practical labor relations.

1. Industrial relations—United States—Addresses, essays, lectures. 2. Personnel management—United States—Addresses, essays, lectures. I. Hoffner, Paul E. II. Gaylor, Robert L. III. Rohaly, Kathleen A.
HD8072.P87 658.3'00973 80-5525
ISBN 0-8191-1119-8

All University Press of America books are produced on acid-free paper which exceeds the minimum standards set by the National Historical Publication and Records Commission.

DEDICATION

This volume is dedicated to:

Robert E. and Sara
Linda
Sally and
Kathryn

for the opportunities, inspiration, guidance, and love they have so selflessly given.

P.E. Hoffner

ACKNOWLEDGMENTS

Publication of this work would not have been possible without the gracious permission of many individuals and organizations to reprint the reading selections contained herein. In addition to the authors specifically identified in the Table of Contents and in the readings, we wish to explicitly acknowledge and express our appreciation to the Center for the Study of Labor Relations, Indiana University of Pennsylvania, and Professor Martin J. Morand, without whose attention and cooperation this project would not have been possible.

We would also like to thank our typists, Ms. Melia Reddinger and Ms. Wendy Neal, for their most important contribution; and, the persons at the University Press of America for all their patience and assistance.

TABLE OF CONTENTS

PREFACE

The labor force in just about every industry is affected by unionism. Either the employees are union members or they depend upon other firms whose employees are unionized. In fact, the labor union today is just as much a part of our society as is the neighborhood shopping center. Unions have both legal status and social approval. They are an integral part of our management scheme an therefore, must be recognized, understood, and worked with effectively.

It is the purpose of this book to provide the reader, especially the reader who is working or plans to enter the world of work in a supervisory capacity, with an exposure to some of the basic concepts of day-to-day labor-management relations. The works of the various authors represent the views of the practitioner, the academician, and the labor expert concerning the important "nuts and bolts" issues today in the field of employee relations.

Although after reading this text you should not consider yourself an expert in labor relations, it is expected that your assimilation of this material will assist you in developing an understanding of some of the practical labor relations skills which will enable you to become a more effective supervisor and/or student of labor-management relations.

I

INTRODUCTION TO POSITIVE LABOR-MANAGEMENT RELATIONS

Traditionally, the relationship between management and labor has been thought of as one of conflict between the boss and the workers. This view has its roots in an earlier period of American industrial history when bosses were the owners of the companies and hired the people to work for them under whatever conditions (wages, etc.) the boss decided upon. While there is certainly historical truth to this view, it is not complete enough to accurately reflect conditions today.

The relationship between management and labor today is characterized by a more cooperative environment. For the most part, either through the collective bargaining process, public policy (laws), or recognition of the importance of the work environment and management style on employee performance, management and labor together determine most of the conditions at the workplace. In some manner or another wage rates are established, job assignments are made, and disagreements and disputes are handled. Although today, as in the past, some companies still attempt to deal with employees on a "take it or leave it" basis, the concept of positive labor relations focuses around the recognition that the key to the attainment of goals which are ultimately of mutual interest - productivity, profits, and an increasingly improved standard of living - lies in the sincere attempt by both labor and management to find acceptable solutions to whatever differences arise.

The readings in this chapter will attempt to introduce the reader to some of the many aspects characteristic of positive labor-management relationships. First, a general examination of the supervisor's individual role in a unionized setting is presented, followed by a graphic illustration of the components in the labor relation process. Third, a discussion of the necessity for labor unions, and finally, a brief view of the nonunion employer.

1.

THE MANAGER AND POSITIVE LABOR RELATIONS

PAUL E. HOFFNER

There are a variety of reasons why employees turn to labor unions. Often times workers view the labor union as a device for assisting them as individuals to achieve such things as higher wages, improved working conditions and a greater voice in organizational decision making. Labor unions also offer psychological advantages to employees through the "strength in numbers" belief--a reality which is best illustrated by the grievance process where employees can voice complaints and/or concerns to management with the full support of the union.

Approximately one-fourth of the labor force in the United States is represented by unions, including an ever growing number of public sector and professional employees, in addition to the more traditional workers in the blue collar industries such as steel, coal and communications. It is clear that since the 1930's the labor union has become a permanent institution in our society. Therefore, it is to the supervisor's or manager's best interest to learn to work with the unions represented in his/her organization.

For many supervisors or managers, a labor union is currently in existence in the organization when they become managers. It is possible, however, that a union-organizing attempt could occur in the organization after the manager has assumed his/her duties. It is important to understand what the manager's general role should be during this effort, for many times it is the managers', both individually and collectively, whose actions become the crucial factors in determining whether or not the employees elect a union to represent them.

Laws governing the union organizing attempt are important but complicated. It is extremely important that managers become familiar with the basic "do's" and "don'ts" of labor law; therefore, a consultation with the personnel or labor relations department should provide the latest legal interpretations.

In general, when a manager is confronted with a union organizing attempt, an immediate report of the activity should be made to top management. While top management will undoubtedly develop a company-wide strategy to deal with the issue, the individual manager should always remember the following:

1. Never threaten workers with reprisals for "talking union."
2. Never promise rewards or special benefits in an effort to influence the worker's choice in electing a union or not.

If or when a union becomes established in the organization for the first time, there will probably be a period of time during which it mav seem difficult for managers to adjust to the new reality. During this time, it is important to <u>recognize and accept</u> the fact that a union does exist and now has the legal right to protect the interests of its members. It is definitely in the best interest of management to encourage a labor-management climate that leads to a cooperative and constructive relationship.

In any efforts to create and maintain a cooperative relationship between labor and management, the individual manager becomes the key to success. Although there is no easy formula for developing a constructive climate, managers must develop the wisdom, sensitivity and respect which illustrate to the workers on a daily basis that the manager views the labor contract as a "living document" and the union as a responsible organization. Since both labor and management must learn to live with each other and deal with mutual problems, the development of a constructive climate, and hence, the individual manager's approach to the reality of unionization, are of vital importance.

Although negotiating the labor contract with the union may be the most visible and perhaps important aspect of the labor-management relationship, the role of the individual manager in this step is usually limited. While negotiations are normally carried out for the organization by a team of persons from top management, managers may be polled for reactions to issues that are most likely to be discussed at the bargaining table. Since many issues raised at the bargaining table by the union relate in some direct way to situations experienced by union members in their daily dealings with individual managers, the managers input into the negotiations process can be valuable in helping the organization's team to prepare strategies and responses to the union's demands. In order to supply this information, managers should always be aware of situations as they arise in their departments and be prepared at all times to substantiate their observations and/or opinions.

The manager's major involvement with the union will take place as the daily interpretation and application of the negotiated labor agreement. While a labor contract does not alter the manager's major duty of directing the workforce under his/her supervision, the manager needs to understand that those managerial duties must be conducted in a way that is consistent with the requirements of the labor contract. It is therefore very important that the manager learn the intended meaning of all of the different sections in the labor contract and apply them accordingly.

In addition, the manager must understand that, under the terms of most labor contracts, employees have the right to challenge or "grieve" managers' decisions if they believe the decision has violated the terms set forth in the labor agreement. In view of this fact, at least one major goal of each manager should be to attempt to make decisions which are fair, unbiased, and consistent with the meaning of the labor agreement, while at the same time not allowing a "challenge" or grievance about a particular decision to upset the manager's confidence or desire to maintain a cooperative, constructive relationship with the union.

Both management and unions alike have learned that it is more productive to live together amicably than to engage in strikes, lockouts and other nonproductive activities. Although there are no easy answers to developing and maintaining a positive labor-management relationship, the role and attitude of the individual manager are clearly at the foundation of the process.

2.

THE LABOR RELATIONS PROCESS

PAUL E. HOFFNER

While the total labor-management relationship consists of the entire scope of dealings between employees and their employers, including hiring, training, on-the-job supervision, compensation, and discipline; the formal or legal concept of labor relations refers to those activities prescribed when management encounters employees wishing to organize a union.

The series of activities presented in Figure 2-1 represent the development and interrelationship of the various components in the formal labor relations process. While none of the activities will be discussed in great detail here, it is important to recognize both the basic focus of each activity and the relationships between the various components.

Beginning with an unorganized workforce, the labor relations process becomes formalized when employees petition for union representation. Various provisions of federal and state law become relevant at this point, and provide specific mechanisms leading to either an election victory and a union's becoming certified as the employees' exclusive bargaining agent or an election loss and the retention of nonunion status. If the employees' votes lead to union recognition and certification, the process then moves to the contract negotiations stage (collective bargaining). Before contract negotiations commence, however, both union and management allow time for adequate preparation of their respective positions and strategies. While the preparation process is vital to success during the negotiation stage, so too does the demeanor and outcome of the negotiating process impact the administration on daily management of the company under the terms set forth in the now present union contract. Although contract administration represents in a sense, the final component in the formal labor relations process, it is as well the beginning of a new cycle of preparation and contract negotation.

Reprinted with permission, Center for the Study of Labor Relations, Indiana University of Pennsylvania, 1979.

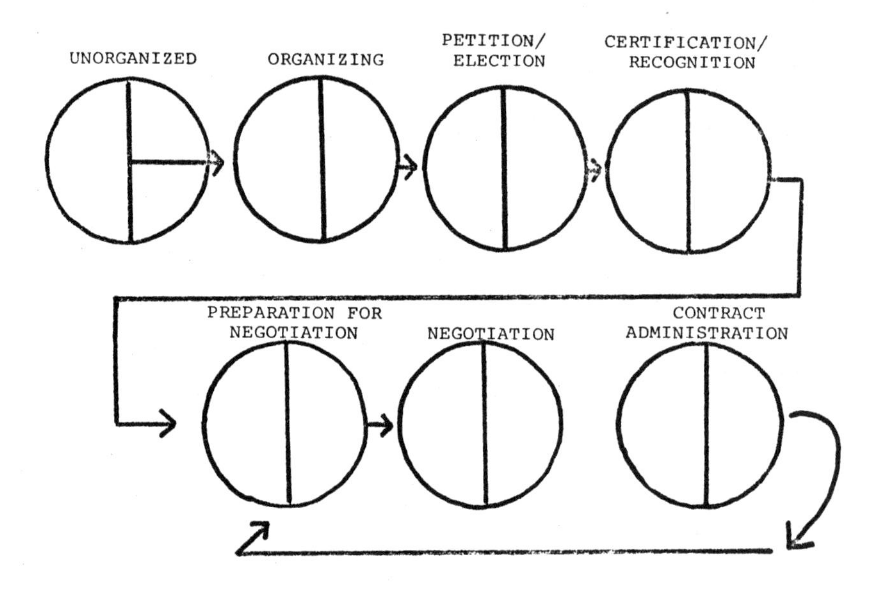

Figure 2-1

3.

"DO WE STILL NEED LABOR UNIONS?"

KENNETH A. KOVACH

It is common knowledge today that organized labor is losing strength in both numerical and political terms, as well as in the influence it exerts over the rest of the labor force. Numerically, labor unions have gone from 42% of the labor force in the 1950's to less than 20% today, with every indication that this downward trend will continue. Were it not for the large number of newly organized public employees, the outlook would be even more ominous for labor unions. And many labor students contend that because of the restrictions on unions in the public sector (many cannot discuss wages and are prohibited from striking), the value to labor as a whole of a certain number of public employees organizing is not nearly as great as a like number of privately employed workers organizing. Thus, even the decreasing numbers may not tell the whole story of labor's deteriorating position.

Losing Clout

Politically, it should be clear to even the most casual observer that unions are losing their clout. The day when the powerful labor boss could "deliver" the labor vote, and hence was admitted to the inner circles of politics and politicians, is gone. It is hard to imagine a modern-day John L. Lewis working closely with the President to draft key pieces of legislation, or inviting congressional leaders to his office to "discuss" their votes on upcoming issues, practices that were once a source of pride and status for powerful labor leaders. Labor's present political influence can best be gauged by their track record on such major issues as the Common Situs Picketing Bill, the original Humphrey-Hawkins Full Employment Bill and Labor Law Reform--all defeats.

While organized labor has long been considered the trend setter for wages and terms of employment, even here we are witnessing the declining strength of unions. Except in a few big industries (steel, auto, etc.) where unions enjoy a virtual monopoly, the increasing number of nonunionized firms have reintroduced the cost of labor as a competitive factor in market strategies. More and more frequently, unions have had to consider the impact of their economic demands on the employers' ability to attract enough business to maintain employment levels. The construction industry is the most dramatic and widely known example of this phenomenon, but it is happening in an increasing number of less publicized instances. The "Southern strategy" of the auto employers, the move to the South of the big steel companies, and the inability of the mining unions to organize new mines are all indicators that even in industries long considered union strongholds, this factor will become increasingly important in the near future.

A Look Backward

The question growing out of the above discussion is obvious. Do we still need labor organizations? Is it not possible that they have outlived their usefulness?

To answer questions such as these, it is important to take a brief look at labor history, which reaffirms one of the more important lessons to be learned from history in general: that if people are pushed hard enough, are subjected to adverse enough conditions, they will take actions they would never have dreamed of had things been more equitable. It is only within the context of the time that today's labor student can understand why otherwise normal individuals would sit in unheated Michigan and Ohio automobile plants in the middle of winter for 42 days, or why they would barricade themselves in steel mills and vow to fight to the death unless working conditions were improved. Read about what workers did to organize the first textile unions, the first mining unions, the first railroad unions, and then ask yourself if you would be willing or able to endure what they did. I contend that you probably could and furthermore that you would probably be willing to if you were subjected to the treatment that those individuals were.

My purpose here is not to discuss the historical plight of the American worker, yet it is crucial to my main point to understand what this plight was. For the first 150 years of this country's independence, the American worker was free politically, but a virtual slave industrially. A look backward at management practices such as company-owned housing, water supplies, stores, etc., with their inflated prices, the payment of workers in company scrip, the unsafe and unhealthy working conditions, the unbelievably long work week, the ridiculously low wages which made it impossible for most families to live on the earnings of a single breadwinner, the completely arbitrary employment and personnel practices, and the company police forces, to mention only a few--in fact the complete lack of consideration of the worker as a human being--puts the remarkable growth of labor unions in the early 1900's in a different light. Certainly at this point in U.S. history, workers were ready to support any type of organization that promised them relief from their miserable industrial existence. Thus, labor unions filled a real need: they brought humanitarianism to the work place and a degree of dignity to the American worker.

Yet ironically enough, because of their success, unions have eradicated most of the conditions that led to their foundation. Thus, an often heard argument today is that while unions were necessary once, they are no longer necessary now. Proponents of this argument content that the American worker today enjoys a higher standard of living than ever before, that we now have laws such as the Fair Labor Standards Act, the National Labor Relations Act, the Occupational Safety and

Health Act, etc., which set a floor for wages, working conditions and general treatment of employees below which no employer is entitled to go.

The Deterrent Effect

While there is much support for this point of view, the author must take exception to it. Laws and subsequent conditions of employment may have changed, but basic human nature has not. While it may be a pessimistic assessment of mankind, and one with which the reader will likely disagree, I firmly believe that a high percentage of humanity will still take advantage of their fellows if the price is right. Over the ages, history has repeatedly proven this to be a truism, and anyone who does not realize it is either uninformed, extremely idealistic or naive. While the laws provide deterrents to employee abuse in the form of minimum acceptable standards, it would certainly be unacceptable to the majority of our working population to exist at those minimum standards. For many, even a small retreat backward, be it in terms of compensation, working conditions or safety standards, would be completely unacceptable. Yet if the law were the only minimum, the only deterrent, there would be plenty of room for retreat in the standards enjoyed in the work place by the majority of the American labor force.

The biggest single deterrent, besides the law, to the reduction of standards in the work place is the combined action of the workers--call it a "union" or any other name you wish. This action does not even have to come to pass to serve its purpose, for in many instances, the mere possibility of such action is sufficient. (There can be no doubt that the level of benefits received by many nonunion workers is in part buttressed by their employers' desire to reward them at such a level that they remain unorganized.)

Thus, while unions may have outlived their usefulness in terms of their original objectives, they are still needed because of what I have been referring to as their "deterrent" effect. If they are in fact the instrument prohibiting exploitation of the worker, not in the traditional browbeaten sense, but in today's more humanistic, less extreme context, then they are in fact needed. The irony is that even those individuals in the blue-collar sector who would suffer first and most if unions disappeared tomorrow don't realize the vital role labor organizations play in today's economy. It is not necessary for them to be as strong as they once were, for the problems they are trying to correct are not as severe, and the government has taken over part of their original role through various pieces of legislation. Yet it is still vital that they continue to exist, not only for those who benefit directly from them, but also for those who believe in the need to maintain the dignity of the worker. Unions find themselves in the same peculiar position as the military, in that what they cause to happen may not be nearly as important as what they cause not to happen. This fact alone, in my opinion, continues to make unions what they've always been--an absolute necessity to the well-being of the work place.

Kenneth A. Kovach, "Do We Still Need Labor Unions?" *Personnel Journal*, December, 1979.

4.

NONUNION EMPLOYMENT

KEVIN JORDAN

One of the most noteworthy facts relating to labor organizations in the United States is the number of employees who do not belong to them. Presently, for every worker represented by a union, there are three who are not. This statistic indicates not so much a decline in union membership as a lack of growth; recent advances in the public sector have not been great enough to offset the leveling trend in the private sector. Luthans and Martinko's suggestion that this ratio presents "resistance"[1] to unionization by those who remain unrepresented may not be entirely accurate, as it implies that the individual has made the choice voluntarily. While this may be the case in some instances, it cannot be considered the principal reason that unionization has not taken place. Along with worker resistance, factors to be considered include worker apathy, fear of management reprisals, lack of information on the part of the workers regarding the mechanics of unionization, size of the organization, and the level of management resistance.

Worker Resistance. A worker's concern that his or her individuality may be comprised through unionization may prompt resistance. American ideals of independence, freedom of action, and self-help cause some employees to opt for a non-union environment. On the other hand, some employees "may not so much prefer individualistic employment relationships as abhor or fear collective ones."[2] Whatever the reason, attempts to thwart union organizational efforts sometimes originate with the workers.

Worker Apathy. It may also be the case that where an attempt to unionize a particular plant or operation is not made by outsiders, workers who have no philosophical objections to unionization simply do not take the initiative themselves. No attempt is made to keep the union out; but neither is one made to bring it in.

Sentiments of this nature may also serve to keep an organizing effort which does originate outside the workplace from picking up the momentum that it would need to result in a successful election.

Fear of Management Reprisals. Regardless of the existence of protections under Federal law of union activities, the fact remains that workers do react to subtle and not-so-subtle management expressions of displeasure with union organizing drives. Management need not utilize blatantly illegal methods; the channeling of a management anti-union position into unofficial lines of communication can be a very effective means of dissuasion.

Lack of Information. Some operations whose workers would be open to the possibility of unionization remain nonunionized because the workers are uninformed with respect to the mechanics involved in the process. This is, of course, most likely to occur where no outside organizer had become involved.

Size. An operation that is likely to remain unorganized in the absence of outside intervention is even more likely to remain that way if its size makes such intervention an improbability. Some operations are so small that the costs to a potential sponsor union in terms of man-hours, possible legal fees, monetary expenditures, etc. will outweigh the anticipated return.

Resistance by Management. The form and intensity of management's efforts to resist an organizing drive will affect the workers' attitudes and behavior toward such a campaign. The net effect of management actions will, however, be the result of the interaction of the other factors which may influence the workers' sentiments toward the union. Aggressive or oppressive behavior on the part of management may serve to kindle a bonfire from what had previously been only scattered embers.

VIEWS ON NONUNION STATUS

According to Dr. Charles L. Hughes,

> Any management that gets a union deserves it -- and they get the kind they deserve. No labor union has even captured a group of employees without the full cooperation and encouragement of managers who create the need for unionization.[3]

Dr. Hughes' rather deterministic view is not, however, universally shared. As Daniel Quinn Mills writes,

> Plants or companies in some industries and geographic areas are likely to be organized no matter what policies the employer follows.[4]

And, conversely,

> In some industries and geographic areas companies can continue to operate much as they did in the 1930's without risk of unionization.[5]

As with the factors which influence employees' views toward unionization, it is likely that there is an interplay of variables related to the employer which will affect union or nonunion status, of which management policies, the industry, and the geographic location are but three.

TYPES OF NONUNION EMPLOYERS

Grouping all nonunion employers together would overstate their similarities. They operate, with respect to the working conditions they provide, on a continuum at whose extremes, according to Mills, are the "low standards" and "better standards" nonunion employers.[6]

Low Standards. A key to the survival of the "low standards" firms is low labor costs. Since such firms are frequently poorly managed, it is imperative that their inefficiently-used labor cost as little as possible in order to preserve their competitive positions in their respective markets. Mills also cites authoritarian management techniques, high turnover, haphazzard personnel practices and the absence of a grievance procedure or communications medium as characteristic of the "low standards" employer.

Better Standards. In contrast, Mills describes the "better standards" nonunion employer as one whose compensation packages and benefits rival or surpass those of comparable unionized firms. Characteristics which may typically be associated with "better standards" management are essentially opposite to those associated with the "low standards" companies; that is, relatively high wages, efficient management techniques, carefully designed and implemented personnel policies, and intricate employee communications networks. Also in contrast to "low standards" firms, "better standards" employers rarely utilize overtly illegal methods to block unionization.

Mills emphasizes that these examples represent the extremes in nonunion environments; between them fall a myriad of combinations of the above-cited dimensions, operating at varying levels and degrees of employer concern -- and disconcern -- for employees. Generally, the intolerable working conditions associated with the "low standards" employers make them likely targets for organizing drives; factors other than employee resistance can be expected to enter into unsuccessful unionization efforts. That is, employees of "better standards" firms are more likely to have remained nonunion of their own volition, whereas employees of "low standards" firms are more likely to be unrepresented due to the influence of external factors. In this vein, Mills assigns considerable weight to the "psychological contract"[7] present in the "better standards" employment situation, through which the employee feels bound in an unwritten, more affective sense to his or her employer.

There is some irony to the fact that, at least in the case of the "better standards" employees, the wage and benefit packages offered by their employer are indirectly the result of union efforts; since these employers deliberately match or beat union gains in an effort to demonstrate that the union is unnecessary, in a sense, the union negotiates the wages and benefits for these nonunion employees. It is, then, the very institution that the "better standards" employees wish to avoid to which favorable working conditions can be attributed.

COMMENTS

Since the enactment of the National Labor Relations Act in 1935, when collective bargaining rights were legally recognized at the Federal level, employers who perceived unionization as a serious and, to some, intolerable infringement on management rights have sought both legally and illegally to circumvent the law. The illegal methods have changed little over time, showing no more and no less imagination than those employes by predecessor employer groups. But the legal methods, as a product of court interpretation, are subject to an entirely separate evolutionary process. The more explicitly the labor policy relating to management tactics in resisting union organizing efforts are defined through court interpretation, the more vividly the route to remaining nonunion and staying within the law is mapped.

FOOTNOTES

[1]Fred Luthans and Mark J. Martinko, The Practice of Supervision and Management, (New York: McGraw-Hill, 1979), p. 278.

[2]Neil W. Chamberlain, Donald E. Cullen, and David Lewin, The Labor Sector (New York: McGraw-Hill, 1980), p. 152.

[3]Dr. Charles L. Hughes, Making Unions Unnecessary (New York: Executive Enterprises Publications Company, Inc., 1976), p. 1.

[4]Daniel Quinn Mills, Labor-Management Relations (New York: McGraw-Hill, 1978), p. 58.

[5]Mills, p. 58.

[6]Mills, p. 49.

[7]Mills, p. 52, referring to M. H. Dunahee and L. A. Wrangler, "The Psychological Contract," Personnel Journal, 53:7, July 1974, pp. 518-526.

II

LABOR LAW

Labor law is simply the total group of legislative enactments (by Congress, state legislatures or administrative agencies such as the National Labor Relations Board) and judicial interpretations (courts) which have either direct or indirect impact on the relationship between employer and employees.

Labor laws have been historically reflective of the emergence of public policy as it pertains to the labor-management relationship. The flow of national legislation shifted over time from repressive laws to a guaranteed right to bargain collectively (Wagner Act, 1935) followed by curbs in the perceived abuses by labor of its relatively new rights (Taft-Hartley, 1947, and Landrum-Griffin, 1959) up to the reality of the enfranchisement of the public sector employee (Federal Executive Orders and state statuses such as Pennsylvania's Act 195 of 1970).

The basic purpose of labor laws is to provide the "ground rules" for the labor-management relationship. While it is not necessary for every supervisor to have a "lawyer's knowledge" of labor law, it is helpful for supervisors to understand some of the major provisions of the various laws.

The first reading in this section provides a brief summary of the major legislation and its judicial interpretation. Reading two provides a discussion of "unfair labor practices"--something of major importance to any organization dealing with a labor union. A discussion of two types of impasse resolution techniques is presented in reading three, and finally, some problems associated with female labor force involvement, and legislative attempts to solve them, are discussed.

5.

AMERICAN LABOR LAW: A CHANGING PHENOMENON

FREDERICK H. NESBITT

The struggle between labor and management in the United States has historically centered around the workers' assertion of their rights to organize and engage in collective bargaining, in the face of an equally vehement assertion by the owners of their right to "manage" without interference. Prior to 1935, this area of conflict fell within the purview of state laws and court decisions, in the absence of a federal law. In 1935, the federal government became involved, with the passage of the National Labor Relations Act (NLRA), an act intended "to diminish the causes of labor disputes burdening or obstructing interstate or foreign commerce." The Act recognized the legitimate differences between labor and management and attempted to institutionalize methods for dealing with these differences. But while its purpose was simple, the NLRA had the effect of shifting the labor-management conflict from the level of individual disputes into the realm of pressure politics, and eventually placed the National Labor Relations Board (NLRB) in a political arena. This attempt to create a set of labor laws that would be uniformly applied was, however, like earlier attempts, unsuccessful in that it, too, was open to inconsistent application.

To fully understand the factors affecting the development of collective bargaining in the United States, it must first be realized that its structure and operation evolved within three distinct yet related environments: political, social and economic.

The political influences of an era unsympathetic to labor were manifest in the frequent issuance of court injunctions against labor activities. In the absence of laws dealing specifically with labor issues and problems, decisions were based on legal precedents set in other contexts. There is little doubt that the judges' inability or unwillingness to accept labor's point of view stemmed, at least in part, from their primarily non-working class socio-economic backgrounds. In addition, the influence of many companies and corporations in the selection and retention of these judges would certainly have entered as a rather compelling factor in their continually making decisions unfavorable to labor. On the wider political front, workers' demands for the institutionalization of collective bargaining through federal law remained unheeded by Congress and the President.

The social environment was dominated by public opinion which was at best non-commital and, at worst, anti-union/anti-collective bargaining. Public opinion did not alter substantially until the 1930's; when the shift finally came, however, it undoubtedly contributed to the passage of the Wagner Act in 1935.

But it was the economic environment that was probably the most dominant of the three. Labor as a whole recognized and accepted capitalism as a viable economic system; at no time did a united labor front advocate the replacement of capitalism in America. Union principles were decidedly in keeping with the "laissez-faire" doctrine, i.e., that the government should not interfere with the free flow of production and consumption. Likewise, under this doctrine, government should not interfere with the right of an employer and employee to negotiate a contract outlining conditions of work, or with enforcement of that contract. This "right of contract" was considered one of the unwritten constitutional rights of a worker. Government involvement in virtually any capacity was seen as interference with this fundamental right. The logical outcome of labor's adherence to these viewpoints was the assumption of antithetical positions by labor and government. Government's lack of support for collective bargaining is, in this context, not surprising.

LABOR LAW: THE COURT INJUNCTION

The absence of a federal labor law did not preclude government involvement in the development of collective bargaining. In essence, the regulation of collective bargaining and the development of labor unions were placed in the hands of the courts, which through their interpretation of legislative efforts, "wrote" labor law up to the 1930's, and have effectively rewritten it since the passage of the NLRA in 1935.

Under the earliest forms of bargaining in the U.S., the question of whether or not a contract would be established between a group of employees (union, association, etc.) and their respective employer was determined by the union's ability to "force" itself on the employer and the employer's ability to counter, or willingness to accept, the union. The relationship was unilateraly lacking the genuine give-and-take of negotiations and bargaining. When there was a contract, it existed until the company eliminated it; that is, the union contract could be unilaterally abolished. However, in 1806, the courts intervened in this relationship. In the case of the Philadelphia Cordwainers, the issue of whether or not a group of employees, organized as a trade association, could join together for the purpose of affecting their wages was addressed. The Philadelphia Cordwainers had struck in 1804 to establish a wage for a pair of boots ($2.75). When the wage was unilaterally lowered, eight cordwainers struck and were subsequently arrested and convicted of illegally conspiring to raise their wages. Thus, the court established the "criminal conspiracy doctrine" under which it was a criminal act for workers to form a labor organization (comination) to benefit themselves (improve wages and conditions of employment). This ruling, based on English common law, placed union organizing activities under criminal law, and made unions themselves illegal. This doctrine was the prevailing labor law during the next 36 years. While it did not result in the massive imprisonment of union members and organizers, it was used most effectively to break strikes and prevent the formation of labor unions.

In the 1840s, the focus of labor law shifted from criminal law to civil law with the decision in Commonwealth vs. Hunt (1842). The Boston Journeymen Bootmakers' Society had a "closed shop" work rule, which resulted in the firing of one worker for failure to pay an initiation fee and for breach of work rules. In the decision that was ultimately handed down, Chief Justice Lemuel Shaw of the Massachusetts Supreme Court held that a combination of workers to improve their working conditions was not a combination in violation of the law. Shaw determined that the possibility of the combination's having a deleterious effect on the employer did not automatically illegalize an otherwise legal, even praiseworthy, collective effort. Thus, the criminal conspiracy doctrine was set aside and workers were able to join and form labor organizations, provided the unions did not directly interfere with an employer's production. Unfortunately, the net effect of this decision was a shift in the courts' emphasis from the criminal conspiracy doctrine to a civil conspiracy doctrine, allowing for broader discretion in the granting of injunctive relief.

The labor injunction was sought by the employer and issued by unsympathetic courts as the labor movement grew during the post-Civil War industrial boom. As industry expanded and labor became scarce, employers added private police forces, strikebreakers, lockouts, blacklists, and the yellow-dog contract to the injunction as weapons to be used against labor. The Pullman Strike of 1894 was a classic example of the use of the injunction in a labor dispute. When the American Railway Union organized a boycott of the Pullman Palace sleeping cars in Chicago, in response to a 30%

unilateral reduction in the wages of Pullman production workers, the court issued an injunction ordering the union to cease and desist from interfering with the transportation of the mail. When the union failed to comply, the President sent federal troops, the boycott was broken, and the union leaders were jailed. Labor in this instance felt the full impact of a labor injunction and judicial repression of collective bargaining. The issuance of labor injunctions, however, served neither to stop the growth of trade unions, nor prevent violence in labor relations.

From the close of the 19th century into the early part of the 20th century, the labor injunction became a favorite weapon of employers, and its use increased dramatically. When Congress passed the Sherman Antitrust Act, it was intended to break up large business monopolies that affected interstate commerce and competition. However, the Court, in the Danbury Hatters Case (1902) interpreted the word "combination" to include the labor union as a "combination in restraint of trade," although the Congressional intent had been application of the law to business combinations. Thus, the customer boycott attempted by the United Hatters was found to be a violation of the law and triple damages were assessed against the individual union members involved, in an amount that exceeded a quarter of a million dollars. When Congress, in 1914, attempted to correct the deficiencies in the Sherman Act through the passage of the Clayton Act, the courts found the new law's language inadequate and returned to the issuance of labor injunctions under the Sherman Act. In this instance, a legislative attempt to correct a judicial misapplication was thwarted, and the <u>de facto</u> labor laws established through court interpretation prevailed.

The intensity of the labor struggle diminished somewhat during the prosperity of the 1920s, although the use of labor injunctions continued to dominate labor law. The great Depression of the 1930s caused changes in the political, social, and economic environments that enabled the country to experiment with new approaches to labor relations. Massive unemployment, low wages, severe working conditions and a perceived threat to American capitalism paved the way for the passage of the Norris-LaGuardia Act (1932). The act was noteworthy in that it was the first piece of federal labor legislation designed to curb the repressive injunctive philosophy of court-made labor law. Its key impact was the severe restriction of court injunctions in labor disputes by the removal of labor from consideration under the Sherman Act. Many states followed suit by passing anti-injunction laws at the state level. In addition, Norris-LaGuardia gave employees the right to join unions and outlawed injunctive relief for violations of a yellow-dog contract.

LABOR LAW: THE BOARD INTERPRETATION

With the passing of the labor injunction, the Roosevelt Administration attempted to promote collective bargaining through Section 7(a) in the National Industrial Recovery Act (NIRA) which guaranteed the right of employees to organize and to bargain with their respective employers. Even before the law could be fully implemented, the Court declared the Act unconstitutional; Congress responded with passage of the National Labor Relations Act in 1935. While the NIRA achieved less than 100% of its goals, unions continued to grow at unbelievable rates, with some more than doubling their memberships. This trend in union growth was paralleled by increasing management resistance.

With the passage of the National Labor Relations Act, Congress and the President decided that labor relations would be conducted by a standard set of rules and regulations, namely, a statutory labor law that placed government in the position of administrator and adjudicator of labor relations matters. This Act, while relatively simple and brief in proportion to its purpose, is based on the federal government's power to regulate interstate commerce; anything affecting or interrupting interstate commerce would fall within the scope of this law. To administer the law, the National Labor Relations Board was created. The NLRB was given the power to conduct representation elections and to prosecute and adjudicate "unfair labor practices" by employers as described in Section 8 of the Act. The heart of the law, however, was Section 7, which described the rights of employees. These rights include joining and forming a union, engaging in collective bargaining and engaging in strike activities; all rights were to be exercised without employer interference. Needless to say, Sections 7 and 8 have been the foci of NLRB decisions and court cases. Each time the NLRB interprets the law and the court sustains or overrules the Board, labor law takes on new and different dimensions.

While the NLRA passed Congress by an overwhelming margin, it did not ease employer resistance. Employers did not accept the law, nor did they drop their opposition to workers' forming unions. In fact, their opposition to organizing campaigns intensified as they waged an assault on the law's constitutionality. Court injunctions effectively suspended the Act until the Supreme Court could address the constitutionality issue. It did so in 1937, in NLRB vs. Jones and Laughlin, where the NLRA was found constitutional. Although this finding forced a shift in the basis for legal arguments, employer opposition continued to take the form of litigation before the Board and in the courts.

After the administration of labor relations had been vested in a single federal agency, it was assumed that labor law application would take on a more constant, stable character. There was as well as assumption of employer compliance with the law through the recognition of democractically elected unions and engagement in good faith collective bargaining. These two expectations proved to be overly optimistic.

From 1935 to 1947, labor law was dominated by Board decisions and court reviews. Unions continued to grow as more employees came to be covered by collective bargaining agreements. Internal problems in the NLRB and external criticism added to the difficulty of the times, as did the suspension of collective bargaining during World War II. The War Labor Board settled disputes, while unions agreed to wage and price controls and no interruption of production. However, at the end of the war, the nation experienced long bitter strikes in most of the major industries. The strikes contributed to a shift in public opinion and a Republican Congress was encouraged to amend the National Labor Relations Act. These amendments, which took the form of the Taft-Hartley bill, were opposed by labor and President Truman. Nevertheless, a coalition of Republicans and Southern Democrats, in response to public opinion, overrode a Presidential veto and passed the Labor-Management Relations Act of 1947.

The amendments were designed to curb "excessive abuses" by labor unions under the original act. Key issues which surfaced during the debate on the amendments included concern over union practices under the original act, a need to reform the NLRB and a need to bring balance to labor-management bargaining. The impact of the amendments was felt in three areas. First, there were changes in the structure of the NLRB. The NLRB was increased from three to five members and was allowed to sit in panels of three; but the most significant change came in the creation of an independent general counsel. This last revision was of special importance because it served to separate the prosecution and adjudication functions of the Board.

Second, application of Section 8 (unfair labor practices) was extended to unions as well as management. Thus, unions were prohibited from interfering with the exercise of employee rights spelled out in Section 7. The amendments recognized three parties in labor relations: management, unions, and the individual employee. The individual's right to join and participate in a union could not be interfered with by either the employer or the union. Third, Section 14 (b) permitted the states to pass right-to-work laws, thus opening the option to the states of outlawing the union shop, while the Taft-Hartley amendments outlawed the closed shop. To some degree, this provision undermined the attempt at the federal level to standardize the practice of labor relations through its allowance for variation at the state level in the legal status of significantly differing collective bargaining philosophies. Today, twenty states have right-to-work laws.

These amendments also contributed to the entrance of labor into partisan politics. The Act prohibited unions from using dues money for partisan political purposes, causing labor to resort to other more direct and more intense political methods to compliment the policy of economic unionism to which it has previously adhered. It was the labor unions who this time turned to the courts in a series of unsuccessful attempts to have sections of the law overturned. From the date of Taft-Hartley's adoption in 1947, neither labor nor business has been able to exert enough influence on Congress to either repeal the amendments or strengthen them. Only in 1959, as a result of Senate hearings into corrupt practices within labor unions, was the National Labor Relations Act amended since Taft-Hartley. The Landrum-Griffin bill, the Labor-Management Reporting and Disclosure Act of 1959, focused on the internal workings of labor unions. These amendments were designed to make the unions more democratic and to maintain consistent internal operating procedures. However, the impact on collective bargaining was not significant.

LABOR LAW: BY PRESIDENTIAL APPOINTMENT AND COURT REVIEW

Finding themselves unable to amend the National Labor Relations Act to their liking, both labor and management began a two-pronged attack in an attempt to influence labor law through (1) NLRB appointments and (2) court appeals of Board decisions.

First, the NLRB came under serious attack. Being unable to eliminate it, or alter it to their liking, both sides attempted to influence Presidential appointments to the Board in an effort to insure decisions favorable to their respective points of view. For example, in 1952, the Republicans captured the Presidency for the first time since the passage of the original Act. Within the first 14 months of the Eisenhower administration, the President was able to appoint three of the five Board members, creating the "Eisenhower Board." Because of the Board's discretionary powers in establishing bargaining units and adjudicating unfair labor practice charges, the new NLRB began to reconsider and reverse policies and practices of the Roosevelt/Truman Boards. In most instances, these decisions favored management, eliciting strong labor objections to many Board rulings. The beliefs and orientations of the Board members were reflected in their rulings.

With the election of President Kennedy in 1960, the Board again took on a new character. Kennedy's first two appointments joined an Eisenhower holdover to form a new majority, thus the "Kennedy Board." This NLRB began reversing decisions from the Eisenhower period in areas such as the scope of bargaining, jurisdiction on classes of workers, free speech for the employer, and picketing procedures. Again, NLRB interpretations resulted in *de facto* amendment of labor law. Today, the Presidential appointment continues to be one mechanism utilized to "create" new labor laws.

As was discussed previously, another extra-legislative means of altering the labor law is through court decisions. All decisions of the NLRB can be appealed to the United States Court of Appeals and finally to the United States Supreme Court. The interplay between changes in dominant

Board philosophies and changes in dominant court philosophies has resulted, at various times since the formation of the NLRB, in periods where Board decisions were repeatedly sustained by the Courts, and periods where the overturn of Board decisions could be predicted with fair accuracy. Most recent history best illustrates this point. In the 1977-78 term of the Supreme Court, the NLRB was consistently upheld by the High Court in every case where the Board was a party. However, during the 1978-79 term, the NLRB was overturned by the Supreme Court in three of four cases involving applications of the NLRA.

So far in 1980, the NLRB is zero for one. The Supreme Court overturned the Board's ruling on private college teachers being covered by the NLRA. The Court ruled that teachers are a part of management, therefore not covered nor protected by the provisions of the Act. In essence, by overturning the NLRB, the High Court has said that the Board has been incorrect in its application of the law for the past ten years.

As a result of Presidential appointments and court decisions, labor law is constantly changing. While the actual law, the National Labor Relations Act, has been formally amended only twice, it has been informally amended thousands of times by different Board majorities and different justices on the Appellate Court and Supreme Court. These labor laws and their applications have created a very structured collective bargaining relationship in the private sector of the economy. Collective bargaining in the public sector is only beginning, although its brief history parallels that of the private sector.

LABOR LAW: PUBLIC SECTOR BEGINNING

Federal and state public sector collective bargaining is relatively new to the field of labor relations. Federal employees were specifically excluded from the provisions of the NLRA by the Taft-Hartley amendments. At the same time, most states were passing laws to prohibit state and local employees from striking. This is not to say that collective bargaining was unheard of in the public sector; rather, that what structure existed was not sanctioned by public sector labor law and that concerted activities, such as strikes, were illegal and subject to court injunctions. It is necessary to separate federal and state employees because of notable differences in the respective governmental jurisdictions.

Federal employees were given the right to collective bargaining by President Kennedy's Executive Order 10899, which allowed federal employees to join and form unions. However, bargaining was restricted to hours and conditions of employment; bargaining over wages and fringe benefits was specifically excluded. The right to strike, which has always been prohibited, was made a felony in 1965, and the union shop was declared illegal. While subsequent executive orders have altered federal sector collective bargaining, the original Executive Order remains the guidelines for federal public sector labor law. With the exception of the postal workers, who were covered by the NLRA in 1970, attempts to bring federal employees under the coverage of the National Labor Relations Act have not been successful.

On the state level, however, considerably more progress has been made in the last ten years. State labor laws range from giving employees the right to join and form unions without the right to negotiate or strike, to giving employees the right to join and form unions, mandatory collective bargaining and the right to strike. The right to strike for essential services, such as policemen and firemen, has been replaced by compulsory binding arbitration. In the 1970s, many state labor laws were passed, with others now under serious consideration. Even states without collective bargaining laws and with no-strike provisions experience collective bargaining relationships and public sector strikes. With the boom of public sector unions and changing public opinion regarding them, labor laws in the near future are likely to focus more and more on questions related to the formation and operation of public sector labor unions.

LABOR LAW: UNFINISHED AMENDMENTS

While the National Labor Relations Act has been amended formally twice and informally thousands of times, four areas of labor law remain under discussion for the 1980's.

First, while the National Labor Relations Act protects the rights of an employee to join a union and engage in collective bargaining, there is no requirement that the negotiations ever lead to a signed contract. As long as negotiations continue in good faith, there is no mandatory termination. Additionally, employees *are* fired for unionization, and have to engage in complicated, expensive litigation to be reinstated. Litigation is also used to delay representation elections, sometimes to the point that a legitimate majority evaporates. The problem is that management can violate the law and only be subject to cease and desist orders and fines. There is no criminal penalty connected with a violation, and, consequently, no real incentive to comply with the law. Legislation to speed up representation elections, give union members greater protection, and require a terminal point to negotiations, i.e., the reaching of an agreement, has failed to pass Congress.

Second, thousands of federal public sector employees remain outside the coverage of the National Labor Relations Act, which in essence prevents meaningful collective bargaining. The debate centers on whether to amend the NLRA and extend coverage to these employees or continue coverage under the 1979 Civil Service Reform Act. There is the additional question of whether or not to allow federal employees to strike or provide an alternative means of settling differences. Unionization of the all-volunteer armed services is contained within this issue.

Third, state right-to-work laws have created inconsistencies in the application of labor law. While there has been only one serious effort to repeal Section 14 (b) (in 1966), the issue continues to be a rallying point for labor and business. The arena for efforts to repeal or legislative right-to-work laws is legislation at the state level, as opposed to the federal level.

The last issue again concerns the federal (and most state) employees. In an attempt to assure that these employees are free of partisan political pressure, they are not permitted to be directly involved in partisan politics. The Hatch Act permits them to exercise their right to vote and participate in public politics, but not to run for party or public office. These "Hatched" employees argue they should be given full political rights, and call for the repeal of the Hatch Act.

LABOR LAW: WHAT IS IT?

Keeping abreast of labor law is a near impossibility; it is being made on a daily and hourly basis. Labor law includes NLRB decisions, court reviews of these decisions, the general counsels' interpretation of the Act, contract administration and arbitrators' awards. Labor law is ever changing as individuals in decision-making positions change. Little did the authors of the National Labor Relations Act and the subsequent amendments realize that such a simply worded and short piece of legislation could be the subject of such great concern and change.

6.

THE LABOR MANAGEMENT RELATIONS ACT NATIONAL POLICY, UNFAIR LABOR PRACTICES AND PROCEDURES OF THE NLRB

DAVID C. WARHOLIC

As President Franklin Roosevelt took office in 1933 during the Great Depression, he promised the nation a New Deal. A basic theory of his New Deal policy was that one of the major reasons for any business depression is the lack of purchasing power among the great body of consumers called workers. Why did the workers lack the power to buy? Roosevelt's administration thought that the low purchasing power was directly attributable to the highly unequal balance of power that existed between labor and management.

In order to remedy the situation, the National Industrial Recovery Act of 1933 was enacted, which, in Section 7, established for employees the right to organize and bargain collectively. It was thought that collective bargaining would provide workers with a powerful device for improving their lowly relationship with management, thus enabling employees to obtain higher wages that subsequently would lead to an increased demand for the goods and services of business.

When the Supreme Court destroyed the NIRA on constitutional grounds in 1935, Congress without hesitation passed the National Labor Relations Act, commonly known as the Wagner Act. However, by 1947, the public had become very critical of the Wagner Act for several practical reasons:

1. The Act allowed all forms of union security, including the closed shop.

2. It made reference to only employer unfair practices.

3. Court interpretation of the Act gave

supervisors the right to form their own unions.

4. The National Labor Relations Board (NLRB) was thought to have a union bias.

These criticisms, coupled with the facts that:

(1) the year 1946 was the worst strike year in the nation's history, and

(2) the public feared a serious post-war inflationary period because of the power afforded labor by the Wagner Act, resulted in the enactment of the Labor Management Relations Act of 1947, more popularly known as the Taft-Hartley Amendments to the Wagner Act.

The amended LMRA is the basis for national labor relations policy as it is applied today. Section 7, the core of the Act, grants employees certain rights that are protected by the unfair labor practice sections. Section 7, which follows, was modified in 1947 so that employees may refrain from union activity as well as engage in it.

> Employees shall have the right to self-organization, to form, join, or assist labor organizations, to bargain collectively through representatives of their own choosing, and to engage in other concerted activities for the purpose of collective bargaining or other mutual aid or protection, and shall also have the right to refrain from any or all of such activities except to the extent that such right may be affected by an agreement requiring membership in a labor organization as a condition of employment as authorized in section 8 (a) (3).[1]

Some examples of employee rights protected by this section are the following:

1. Forming or attempting to form a union among the employees of a company.

2. Joining a union regardless of whether or not the union is recognized by the employer.

3. Going on strike to secure better working conditions.

4. Assisting a union to organize the employees of an employer.

A second modification in 1947 was the addition of unfair practices to be applied to unions. A list of some of the more common <u>unfair labor practices by unions</u> follows:

1. Mass picketing that bars nonstriking employees from entering the work site.

2. Violent acts on the picket line, or in connection with a strike.

3. Fining employees after they have resigned from the union for acts of misconduct.

4. Threats to employees that they will either lose their jobs or be physically hurt unless they join the union.

5. Threats to do bodily injury to non-striking employees.

6. Either fining or expelling union members for filing charges with NLRB.

7. Declining to process a grievance for an employee because the employee criticized the union or its officers.

8. Contracting with an employer to represent the employees when the union was not selected by a majority of the employees.

9. Forcing an employer to recognize the union when actually another union has been certified by the NLRB to represent the employees.

10. Refusing to meet with the person the company has engaged as its representative in contract negotiations.

11. Fining or expelling supervisors who are members of the bargaining unit for the manner in which they apply the contract while performing their supervisory functions.

12. Forcing an employer to reduce the seniority of an employee because the individual engaged in anti-union behavior.

13. Refusing to negotiate on a proposal for a written contract.

14. Refusing to process a grievance because an employee is not a union member.

15. Terminating a contract and striking for a new one without notifying the employer and the Federal Mediation and Conciliation Service.

16. Picketing an employer in an effort to force it to cease doing business with a second employer who will not recognize the union.

17. Asking employees not to work with equipment manufactured by a nonunion company.

18. Refusing to bargain in good faith with an employer.

19. Striking an employer to compel it to bargain separately when the company has bargained, and continues to bargain, on a multiemployer basis.

20. Creating a contract that forces an employer to hire only union members.

21. Charging union members excessive or discriminatory fees when they are required by a union-shop agreement to be members of the union.

The following is a list of unfair labor practices for employers:

1. Questioning of employees concerning their union views prior to a board election.

2. Withholding of a promised but unspecified wage increase during a union organizational drive.

3. Stating that the employer had previously closed a business rather than bargain with a union.

4. Threatening to close down the business if the employees vote for a union.

5. Threatening employees with loss of jobs or benefits if they join or vote for a union.

6. Making campaign speeches to assembled groups of employees on company time during the twenty-four hour period before an election.

7. Spying or pretending to spy on employees when assembled for union purposes.

8. Giving wage increases intentionally timed to discourage employees from joining or forming a union.

9. Organizing a union or a committee to represent the employees.

10. Giving one of several unions trying to

represent employees the right to solicit on company property, or other privileges, and denying other unions the same privilege.

11. Discharging employees because they joined a union or urged other employees to join.

12. Refusing to reinstate an employee because he testified at an NLRB hearing.

13. Refusing to reinstate employees when jobs they are qualified for are open, because they took part in a union's lawful strike.

14. Closing an operation at one plant and discharging the employees while reopening the same operation at another plant with new employees because the employees at the initial plant joined a union.

15. Refusing to hire qualified applicants for jobs because they either belong to a union or did not belong to a union.

16. Refusing to bargain with the employees' representative because the employees are out on strike.

17. Unilaterally announcing a wage increase.

18. Refusing to meet with employees' representatives to bargain mandatory subjects, i.e. pensions, bonuses, safety practices grievance procedures, seniority, discipline, union security, etc.

19. Firing an employee because the individual gave adverse testimony at an NLRB hearing.

20. Causing incitement of racial or religious prejudice by inflammatory campaign appeals.

National Labor Relations Board Procedures:

In order for the NLRB to become involved with a particular case, a charge must be filed with the Board either against an employer or a union or both. A union, employer, employee, or other person may file charges.

After charges are filed, a field examiner from the local regional office of the NLRB investigates its validity. During this investigation, the charges may be adjusted, withdrawn, dismissed, or otherwise closed without formal action.

A formal complaint will be issued by the regional director, if the investigation shows the charges are substantiated by the facts and the case is not settled by adjustment. An "adjustment" means that the Regional Office has reached an agreement with the charged party that it will modify the action or inaction which resulted in the charge.

If a complaint is filed, a date is issued for a hearing before a trial examiner. The trial examiner will preside like a judge, listening to witnesses presented by the parties and receiving evidence. He/she will then issue a written decision of his/her findings and recommendations.

A party may appeal the trial examiner's decision to the Board's central office in Washington, D.C. Unless either of the parties files a statement of exceptions to the judge's findings within 20 days, the recommended order takes the full effect of the NLRB. If appealed, the Board itself will review the case and issue a decision and order. A party who objects to the NLRB's decision may then appeal to an appropriate U.S. court of appeals.

If the accused party is found to have committed an unfair labor practice, the board will order it to post notices informing the employees that it has committed an unfair labor practice and that it will refrain from such violations in the future. In addition, the NLRB has the power to order an employer to make whole any employees who have suffered a loss of earnings because of the employer's discrimination in violation of the Act.

In short, the unfair labor practice provisions of the NLRA comprise a tool for channeling employer and union actions towards constructive ends. The fact that both parties usually recognize and respect the prescribed actions helps to provide a more conducive, positive environment for the labor-management relationship.

FOOTNOTE

[1]National Labor Relations Act; Section 7.

7.

TWO APPROACHES TO IMPASSE RESOLUTION

KATHLEEN A. ROHALY
PAUL E. HOFFNER

An "impasse" is defined as a point in time when labor and management are deadlocked in their discussions with no additional prospect for compromise or no resolution apparent. Although impasses are certainly not uncommon in labor relations, it is evident that minimization of the number and duration of such occurrencies can aid in the establishment or maintenance of the cooperative environment which is prerequisite to a positive labor-management relationship.

Generally, an impasse occurs at one of two points in the labor-management process. First, if during the negotiation of the collective bargaining agreement, neither side is willing to alter its position on some integral issue or issues, making further compromises in an effort to avoid deadlock an impossibility, impasse is said to have been reached. The historical response to an impasse at this point is a work stoppage, a strike or lockout. While these options may have the short-run effect of breaking the impasse, they can ultimately contribute to the deterioration of the total positive labor-management relationship.

Secondly, impasses can occur during the administration of the negotiated agreement. These situations arise when labor and management are unable to resolve grievances or disputes through traditional grievance procedures. As an alternative to the work stoppage, the grievance procedure has generally been expanded to include binding arbitration as a more positive impasse resolution technique.

Presented below in Figure 2-1 are two major impasse resolution techniques. The special demands and requirements peculiar to each unique situation will be the variables around which a decision must be made regarding the appropriateness of a particular impasse technique. What is of critical importance here, however, is the recognition that through the utilization of procedures of this nature, labor and management have a vehicle for the amicable resolution of disputes without the deleterious effects of a work stoppage.

TYPES OF IMPASSE RESOLUTION

	Mediation	Arbitration
Process	Intervention by Federal Mediation and Conciliation Service or other appropriate neutral whose involvement has been requested and/or accepted by the negotiating parties.	A terminal procedure, an alternative to or following factfinding, usually final and binding
Subject Matter	Negotiation of terms of agreement.	Negotiation of terms of agreement; final step in grievance procedure.
Method	Mediator tries to determine basis for agreement and persuade parties to reach agreement	Parties try to persuade arbitrator by arguments (same as factfinding) to get favorable decision.
Third-party	Mediator - A Federal Commissioner of Mediation and Conciliation or other third party.	Arbitrator - a public employe or a private citizen selected by parties or by an administrative body.
Power Factor	Mediator limited to persuasion and ability to find compromise.	Arbitrator makes binding decision.
Publicity	Confidential process - no public record kept.	Quasi-public process with decisions recorded and reported.

Figure 2-1

8.

BUT CAN SHE TYPE?

KATHLEEN A. ROHALY

The world in which the American working woman finds herself is a man's world. Women have traditionally found employment in the secondary labor market. Aspirations toward serious, career-minded occupations are viewed as anything from quaint to absurd to anti-social. The resultant, self-perpetuating cycle of opportunities not offered and opportunities not sought represents a serious waste of valuable human resources.

Yet, in spite of the obstacles, the challenge is being accepted by increasing numbers of women. Whether the motivation is pragmatic or philosophical, a deep commitment by persons of both sexes has been the impetus behind ever-widening inroads into previously limited job opportunities.

Recent Trends

There is little doubt that the number of female workers in the U.S. is on the rise; in fact, it is estimated that as much as two-thirds of the increase in labor force participation in the last decade can be attributed to women. Almost half of the adult female population in the U.S. is working, and two out of every five workers are women.[1]

The growth of industry in general, but of service industries (an area affording the part-time employment situations appealing to many women) in particular, has provided expanded opportunities for greater numbers of Americans seeking to enter the work force. Women are choosing to participate primarily for the same reasons as men--economic ones. There are indications that the belief that women work purely voluntarily is exaggerated.[2] They are working to support, in whole or in part, themselves and/or their families.

But an equally, if not more, important aspect of women's entrance into the work force is the role of social change in the upsurge. Among key social factors are:

> . . . society's increasing acceptance of working mothers; delay or postponement of having children by married couples in their twenties; fewer children, smaller family units; more single (never married) women choosing to keep and raise their own children;. . .exceedingly high rate of broken marriages; and no-fault divorce legislation in some states. . .[3]

Part of what these trends indicate is that not only is it becoming acceptable for women to work, but in more and more cases it is becoming necessary. In 1972, about 12% of all American families were headed by women;[4] in 1978, there were some 5.7 million single-parent families in the U.S. and

> [f]or the most part, one-parent families were maintained by mothers; only 540,000 were maintained by fathers and they only rarely faced the economic difficulties encountered in families with a mother only.[5]

The consensus appears to be that mothers of young children represent the most significant addition in recent times to the work force.[6] "In Europe and in the United States, the most rapidly growing group is composed of mothers with preschool children."[7] These women's circumstances are such that part-time work is for them most feasible. Typically, however, such work offers little by way of current rewards, advancement, or long term security.

Two related observations are apparent from even the most cursory examination of the female work situation. First, women as a group earn less money then men. Estimates are that, overall, salaries of female wage earners are about 60% those of male workers. Secondly, women remain concentrated in low prestige white collar jobs primarily in sales, clerical and service occupations. Few women enter professional and technical fields and even fewer become managers and administrators. There is some speculation that women are more willing--and able--than men to forfeit monetary gains in order to derive other benefits from employment, such as flexible hours, closeness to home or even simply the chance for a change of environment. The greater likelihood, however, is that the exchange is not deliberate.

Legislative and Judicial Context

Within the last two decades, recognition of the problems associated with female participation in the labor force has taken the form of special legislation designed to minimize obstacles and maximize opportunities. In some instances sex discrimination has been specifically addressed; in others, it has been included as one dimension of discrimination in general.

Among initial legislative efforts at the federal level was the Equal Pay Act of 1963. The Act illegalized the practice of payment of different wage rates to males and females whose jobs were essentially equal in the amount of effort and skill required to perform them, had basically the same responsibilities, and were performed under the same conditions. Correction of violations by decreasing the higher rate to the level of an improperly paid lower wage level was not acceptable.

Sex discrimination was also one area dealt with in Title VII of the Civil Rights Act of 1964. The Act forbade discrimination based on sex, race, national origin, religious beliefs, or color by employers and employment agencies, as well as unions. In addition, it created the Equal Employment Opportunity Commission (EEOC), although the Commission was at that time given no powers of enforcement. Title VII coverage was broadened in 1972, with the passage of the Equal Employment Opportunity Act which, in addition, provided for enforcement of EEOC decisions through the courts.

Also at the federal level, Executive Order 11246 (as amended in 1968 by Executive Order 11375) forbade discrimination in employment along Title VII dimensions by government contractors who met certain criteria. In 1971, the Secretary of Labor issued "Revised Order 4" which compelled prime government contractors to set up definitive goals and timetables for the movement of females into their work forces at all levels, under threat of the loss of their government contracts.

There have also been numerous legislative enactments at the state level dealing with the employment of females. Some states have passed laws which afford women special "protections" such as restrictions on the number of hours per day or time of day that they may work. Such laws, however, have frequently had the effect of imposing severe limitations on female employment opportunities or job related benefits; the proscriptions cited above, for example, would serve to exclude or restrict overtime opportunities for women or preclude the possibility of a night-shift wage differential for female workers. Other state laws, requiring special benefits such as rest periods or the availability of physical facilities for women, have resulted in employer unwillingness to assume the added expense associated with female workers and consequently have affected hiring practices. However, the EEOC has stated in its guidelines that adherence to these types of laws is not a basis for a defense in a discrimination charge, since the EEOC considers such laws to be in conflict with Title VII of the Civil Rights Act; this view has generally been upheld by the courts.

As in other areas of law, statutes dealing with sex discrimination have been vitalized through court interpretation. Such issues as height and weight restrictions, differing grooming standards for men and women, placement of jobs in classified ads under "male" and "female" headings, and differences in benefits offered to male and female employees and/or their spouses, have been recent subjects for litigation. A critical factor in many decisions, especially those related to hiring or differential payment policies, has been whether or not the practice can be shown to relate to a "bona fide occupational qualification" (BFOQ). The Supreme Court has stated that a crucial element in establishing the existence of such a qualification is whether or not the contested requirement is "demonstrably more relevant to job performance for a woman than for a man."[8]

An issue of special concern to women that has been the focus of much attention in the courts in recent times is childbirth and its implications in the areas of job performance, benefits, leave allowance, seniority accrual, sick leave or disability payments, etc. Since its applicability to males and females is inherently unequal, it has proven to be a rather sensitive issue. The courts have had no small task in attempting to balance demands for provision of special considerations to persons whose work force participation is significantly affected by childbirth, with accusations of *de facto* denial of those same considerations to persons whose work force participation is not or will never be affected by childbirth. Like many trends in judicial interpretation, court decisions on these questions are likely to reflect changes in social perceptions and, thus, can be expected to vary with variations in public sentiment.

Implications and Conclusions

Women are in the labor market to stay. The "declining birth rate, the substitution of capital and other labor saving services for those of the mother, and the increase in women's wages over time"[9] will continue to contribute to greater female involvement in the labor market.

It is likely that attempts will be made to overcome the mechanical problems associated with female participation such as providing more day-care facilities or adjusting hours or days of work, but efforts might be more prudently expended on the deeper issues. There may be a tendency to focus on the problems of the individual without dealing with the wider, more serious social and economic implications.

The greatest obstacles to females who wish to pursue careers are the social barriers. Popular thinking which characterizes the female as the homebound figure whose labor force participation is secondary in nature and importance will not easily be altered. Women who _do_ work do so at their own risk; they are expected to continue to assume home responsibilities in addition to their outside jobs, almost at the same levels as women who do not work outside of the home.

The tendency to view what _is_ as what should or must be prevails with reference to male/female roles, and a concerted, focused effort must be made if present attitudes are to change. Females who aspire to "male" careers and job fields should not be forced to play the role of the trouble-making malcontent.

The influx of mothers of young children into the work force has raised and will continue to raise some interesting questions. The concept of primary care during the "formative" years by a person or persons other than the mother is still something of a revolutionary one. Predictions of what effect--if any--this factor may have on a child's psychological and emotional development are as yet varied and inconclusive.

In 1973, the AFL-CIO convention endorsed the Equal Rights Amendment. But an interesting dilemma for labor unions--presently male-dominated--is presented by such a policy. As Anne Nelson writes,

> [t]he central political problem labor has

> in representing women's employment interests is that it also represents the people who already have the jobs to which women are beginning to aspire.[10]

While legislative efforts such as the Equal Pay Act of 1963 are steps in the right direction, much more needs to be done. Equal pay without equal access is only part of the answer.

The lack of power of the female working population in proportion to women's numbers is due in part to the non-strategic employment positions held by women, but more importantly to the under-representation of females in legislative, judicial, managerial, administrative and other "power" positions. As long as traditionally minded individuals remain the policy makers, women will face an uphill climb.

FOOTNOTES

[1]Carolyn J. Jacobson, "Women Workers: Profile of a Growing Force," American Federationist, July 1974, p. 9.

[2]Alice Cook, The Working Mother: A Survey of Problems and Programs in Nine Countries (New York State School of Industrial and Labor Relations, 1978), p. 5.

[3]Elizabeth Waldman, et al, "Working Mothers in the Seventies," Monthly Labor Review, 102:10, October 1979, p. 39.

[4]Jacobson, p. 9.

[5]Waldman, et al, p. 45.

[6]Jacobson, p. 10; Waldman et al, pp. 40-41.

[7]Anne Nelson, "The One World of Working Women," Department of Labor, Bureau of International Affairs, Monograph No. 1, (U.S. Government Printing Office, Washington, D.C., August 1978), p. 2.

[8]Phillips vs. Martin Marietta Corporation, 3 FEP Cases 40 at 41.

[9]Richard Morgenstern and William Hamovitch, "The Labor Supply of Married Women in Part-time and Full-time Occupations," Industrial and Labor Relations Review, Volume 30, No. 1, October 1976, p. 59, referring to Jacob Mincer, "Labor Force: Participation II in David L. Sills, ed. International Encyclopedia of Social Sciences, Volume 8 (New York: Macmillan, 1978), pp. 474-81.

[10]Nelson, p. 12.

III

PREPARING AND NEGOTIATING THE COLLECTIVE BARGAINING AGREEMENT

Negotiation is a process whereby labor and management confer with the intent of reaching an agreement. This fundamental concept is set forth as a requirement of section 204 of the Labor Management Relations Act, 1947 (Taft-Hartley). But the simplicity of the term's definition does not reflect the complexities involved in the implementation of the process.

Negotiation is rooted in communication. In the labor relations setting it is the interaction of certified representatives of employee groups with their managerial counterparts.

As collective bargaining relationships have matured and become increasingly sophisticated, so has the negotiation process. It is not simply smoke-filled rooms or fists banging on the tables. It is replete with the nuances of psychological analysis and power strategies.

Those who are prepared to negotiate--who have done their "homework"--will be ahead of their competition. Success at the bargaining table may be determined by the negotiator's ability to both make accurate assumptions of his/her own party's needs as well as anticipate the assumptions on which the other side is relying.

The labor management negotiation is generally carried on under at least two significant threats, one from each side of the table: management's ability to lock out, go out of business or relocate; and labor's ability to strike. Negotiators understand clearly the consequences of their failure to achieve a settlement.

The readings in this section are intended to give you some flavor of the processes involved, some "while bargaining" basics, and some of the concerns of management over the always present possibility of employee strikes, should an impasse occur.

9.

BARGAINING BASICS

PAUL E. HOFFNER
KATHRYN L. HOFFNER

Collective bargaining is the process of group decision making between labor and management. The purpose of collective bargaining is to arrive at a mutually acceptable body of rules (i.e. contract) to enable labor and management to work in a productive relationship. While it is important to recognize the formal components of the process utilized at the table, an understanding of the "bargaining basics" or informal process/techniques, is necessary to make collective bargaining a success.

Presented in an outline form as suggested by the Labor-Management Services Administration[1], basics are intended only to provide the manager with a cursory view of the process in order to enable a more complete understanding and acceptance of the benefits of a positive collective bargaining relationship.

I. The Contract

A. A Body of Rules

1. The contract is the result of negotiations between the management of an enterprise or representatives of management and representatives of its employees.

2. The negotiations set up rules, agreed to by both labor and management, which cover broadly wages, hours, and working conditions.

3. The rules are set down in writing. This coding of the agreed rules is the contract. The contract is a treaty for industrial peace between employee and employer.

B. Enforceable

1. The contract prescribes its own rules for enforcement (usually through arbitration), modification, and renewal.

2. The rules are enforceable in courts, in varying degrees.

3. How strictly a contract can be enforced will depend greatly on how many ways the rules may be interpreted.

4. The number of ways in which a rule, or contract clause, may be interpreted will depend upon how clearly and how carefully the clause is worded and the terms defined.

C. Different from a Contract to Purchase Something

1. The collective bargaining contract does not compel any individual to work and does not commit management to hire or retain an individual except under certain conditions.

2. It merely lays down the rules which govern the relationship:

a. if the employer hires workers, and

b. if the employees are willing to work for the employer.

II. Preparing to Negotiate a Contract

A. Selection of a Negotiation Committee - Labor and Management

1. The members in the bargaining unit may elect the bargaining committee. Management will select a committee comprised

of persons such as Personnel Director, Comptroller, Chief Negotiator, etc.

B. Forming Positions

1. The union's stewards can communicate the workers' major goals and sources of friction to the negotiation comittee. Management will rely on supervisors' opinions, research of other contracts and the business/economic forecasts to help them in forming their positions.

2. For both parties, the records in grievance cases will sometimes reveal weak spots in the contract.

   a. They may indicate where the contract is poorly worded, allowing for a different interpretation of clauses than the parties intended.

   b. They may indicate trouble areas not covered by the present contract.

   c. They may indicate areas where the contract did not accomplish what it was intended to accomplish. (Example: a poor seniority clause--the union thought it would work, but it didn't.)

C. Be ready to back up the proposal at the bargaining table.

1. Get the necessary facts--this means much in-depth research.

2. Both parties will try to anticipate the position of the party on the other side of the bargaining table on controversial issues.

III. Initiating the Negotiations

A. The time for the Meeting.

1. If negotiations are held during working hours, the problem arises as to who pays committee members for lost time. Usually the union local pays its team members their regular rate of pay, while the management team members are considered to be at work.

2. Negotiations may be held after working hours so that lost time is not a factor.

B. The Setting

1. It is usually desirable to have a place that is neat and pleasant. Possible locations are:

    a. Union conference room.

    b. Management conference room.

    c. A hotel meeting room.

2. A neutral place is sometimes desired.

    a. This would tend to rule out both the union and management locations.

    b. The cost of the meeting place would be shared by the parties.

C. The First Meeting

1. Proposals may have been exchanged prior to the first meeting or at an informal pre-negotiation conference.

2. The first meeting is an explanatory one.

    a. Proposals are exchanged.

b. Procedure is planned.

c. Time and place for the next meeting is agreed upon.

IV. Collective Bargaining - While collective bargaining generally is the process of seeking agreement, from the parties' standpoints it is the process of seeking agreement by persuading the other side to accept your point of view.

A. Looking at the Contract as a Whole.

1. What do the proposals of the company and the union have in common? What are the points of agreement?

2. What are the points of least controversy? On what points may the differences be settled easily? These points may be settled first. The parties should seek to create an atmosphere of agreement early in the negotiations.

B. Settling Disagreements.

1. Some issues may be considered individually.

a. Examination of each demand individually encourages examination of each issue on its merits.

b. It discourages "horse trading."

c. It may preserve the "atmosphere of agreement."

d. The "basket approach" or "horse trading" approach in bargaining for a total settlement may lose sight of the implications of individual proposals and might encourage careless wording and invite later conflicts over interpretation.

2. Some issues are interrelated and must be considered in relation to each other.

   a. Some issues cannot be considered by themselves and must be considered as part of the whole. Money outlays are an example. Direct wage increases cannot always be considered apart from fringe benefits. The company must consider the total money cost.

   b. If the proposal asks for a shorter work week at increased pay, the wages and hours issues become related.

   c. Concentration on individual issues may cause the parties to lose sight of the overall objectives of the contract.

3. Some of the arguments will be factual and some arguments will be emotional.

   a. Facts must be countered with facts.

   b. At the bargaining table, facts support the arguments on each side and facts may also answer the arguments on the opposite side of the table.

   c. Emotional arguments usually fall flat when countered with facts.

4. The committee should plan its negotiating strategy before each meeting.

5. The spokesman should keep the committee united.

    a. Committee members should never disagree among themselves at the bargaining table.

    b. When there are doubts about the committee's unity, the meeting should be adjourned for separate discussion.

C. Reporting back to the Members

1. The attitude of the members toward the negotiations is a bargaining weapon. The object from the union's point of view is to arouse the vocal support of the membership to back up their committee while not expecting more than the committee anticipates that it will have to settle for.

2. In the final settlement, both sides may have to agree to something different than they originally expected or demanded.

3. Reports should be made only at regular or special meetings, the committee should agree on what to tell the members, and the members should not be told any idle gossip nor any conflicting information.

V. Tactics and Techniques

A. At the table

1. Ask questions

    a. Gain insights into the other party's point of view.

b. Get an indication of the arguments they will use.

2. Be honest

   a. Know what your're talking about.

   b. Don't pad the facts.

   c. "Blue-sky bargaining" creates mutual distrust.

   d. Honesty commands respect which invites an "atmosphere of agreement."

3. Don't horse trade until the very last. Try to settle the issue on merit first.

4. Mutual respect is essential at the bargaining table.

   a. When a spokesman on the other side makes a rash statement, it is better to not make him look foolish by answering him.

      (1) It is usually best to help him save face by explaining that you know him well enough to know that he doesn't mean it.

   b. Don't challenge the integrity of the opposing team.

   c. Mutual respect means the Golden Rule.

      (1) Give the respect you expect to receive.

5. The right to strike is a silent member of every negotiating committee.

a. Its chief effectiveness is the knowledge that it can be used.

b. A threat to strike is usually not used at the bargaining table.

c. When negotiations drag out too long, a strike vote is taken as a matter of course, and usually some time before strike action is expected to take place.

    (1) A strike vote usually carries with it the authorization for the executive board or officers to decide when action is to take place.

d. Negotiations will never be helped by idle strike threats.

e. Both sides must calculate the cost of a strike.

    (1) What are the chances for victory?

    (2) How much will be gained?

    (3) How long will it take?

FOOTNOTE

[1]Instructor's Guide, Settle or Strike, Labor-Management Services Administration, U.S. Department of Labor, 1973.

10.

PREPARING FOR EMPLOYEE STRIKES

PAUL E. HOFFNER

Collective bargaining is a process of shared decision-making, the outcomes of which are based to a large extent on the power relationships of the parties. The employee strike or work stoppage is one of the key elements in affecting these power relationships, and hence, the outcome of negotiations.

While it is not the purpose of this article to suggest that strikes are either inevitable or necessary, it is suggested that good management engaged in the practice of positive labor relations still must recognize that the possibility of a strike always exists; therefore, adequate preparation is not only necessary, but wise as well.

Successful planning for the possibility of employee work stoppages consists of at least two levels of thinking. On the first or conceptual level, the manager must confront and attempt to deal with such realities as:

1. The possibility of work stoppage occurring under present/future conditions.
2. The value of the strike plan as a bargaining tool in the negotiation process.
3. The level of preparation for a work stoppage by the employee organization.
4. The willingness and ability of the company to encounter a work stoppage.
5. The consequences of less than adequate preparation for the work stoppage.

On the second or operational level, the manager must, in concert with other members of the management team, develop a plan of action which attempts to anticipate and provide solutions to the daily difficulties of maintaining operations under strike conditions. Such a plan should include, in the view of Lee T. Paterson and John Liebert in their Management Strike Handbook[1], at least the following:

- --Establish strike plan committees, which, under direction of Chief Executive/Administrative Officer, coordinates development and implementation of plan
- --Provide for appointment of strike coordinator
- --Establish on-going public and employee communications vehicles, which can then be used if and when strike occurs
- --Review personnel policies, and modify or draft and have ready emergency rules/resolutions
  - --Leave of absence rules
  - --Continuance of group insurance benefits
  - --Interruption in accruing credit for purposes of retirement, paid leaves such as vacation and sick leave, time in grade for purposes of probationary period, promotion and seniority in general
  - --Treatment of striking employees who are on authorized leave when strike begins or are scheduled to commence during strike, or who become sick during time of strike
  - --Obligation re "paid holidays" that occur during strike
  - --Review job specs to make sure all duties covered (in event of slow-down actions)

--Establish relative essentiality factors by facility, job classification, position, location and shift on agency-wide basis

--Emergency staffing
  --Plan, position by position, which functions at which facilities must be staffed to maintain varying levels of decreased operations down to minimum acceptable level
  --Determine position by position alternate staffing for varying levels of decreased operations (departmental and non-departmental management, supervisory and other non-representative unit personnel on an individual basis, and non-agency sources)
  --Develop training to be conducted periodically for substitute employee "task forces"
  --Provide for and/or review mutual aid arrangements with other public agencies
  --Arrange for potential private subcontracting (refuse collection, private security firms, emergency maintenance, custodial)
  --Review licenses required for operating essential equipment and vehicles and assure that adequate licensed personnel will be available among departmental and non-departmental substitute people

--Emergency Communications
  --Special unlisted telephone lines to key locations and officials
  --Use of two-way radios
  --Establish stand-by courier service
  --Maintain emergency telephone list of key officials
  --Special phone line to notify non-striking employees where and when to report for work

--Security
- --Arrangements for visible uniformed police protection (public agency and/or private security) for non-strikers crossing picket lines, agency buildings and facilities (key locations on round-the-clock basis), and homes of top agency officials
- --Develop list of control valves, switches, control centers, alarm boxes, communications equipment and other critical installations (for use by security personnel)
- --Plan for a system of identification passes for operation personnel who will be authorized to enter facilities containing such critical equipment
- --Have available in strike headquarters duplicate supplies of keys to facilities and equipment
- --Have stand-by arrangements with locksmith service (to change locks), emergency plumbing service, garage and window repair services
- --Security planning should emphasize such sensitive locations as picket lines, entrances to key agency buildings, strike headquarters, communications center, agency public utility facilities and employee parking lots
- --Arrange for collection from employees going on strike of all agency equipment (keys, tools, etc.)

--Emergency supplies
- --Stocking of essential operating supplies (e.g., chemicals for water and sewage treatment plants)
- --Arrange for live-in facilities for key personnel (food, sanitation, and bedding)

Planning for a strike is not an easy process, but the necessity to consider such a possibility and be prepared for it far outweighs the costs of the planning itself. At worst, adequate planning can serve the function of decreasing the tendency of the employee organization to consider a work stoppage - knowing that management is fully prepared. At best, the existence of a strike plan may make it clear to both labor and management, that the place to settle contract negotiation disputes or disagreements is at the bargaining table and not on the picket lines.

FOOTNOTE

[1] Lee T. Patterson and John Liebert, *Management Strike Handbook*, Chicago: International Personnel Management Association, 1974, pp 38-39.

Reprinted with permission of the author.

IV

CONTRACT ADMINISTRATION AND THE GRIEVANCE PROCESS

Contract administration is the stage of the collective bargaining process where union and management will spend the majority of their time. For the term of that agreement, the parties must live by the provisions they have negotiated.

Successful administration of the agreement is rooted in uniformity and consistency. Without these factors, the parties cannot possibly have a harmonious relationship. Without harmony, there is no stability. The result will inevitably be a significant level of grievances and other labor relations problems.

Yet, in spite of labor and management's best efforts and no matter how carefully an agreement is written, problems will arise. No contract can hope to cover all the contingencies in the workplace. To provide for such eventualities, a dispute resolution mechanism is normally a part of the contract. A grievance procedure ending in binding arbitration is the standard methodology.

A grievance procedure permits the following:

A clear opportunity for the employee to air complaints and for those complaints to be addressed.

A rational method of channeling conflict without significant disruption to the parties; i.e., a "steam vent."

An opportunity for employee-management communication that should alert management to problem areas.

A structure through which the union can enforce the terms of the agreement.

A forum through which the ambiguities in an agreement can be clarified.

Ideally, the parties will learn to solve problems at the lowest possible levels of the grievance process. This will not always be possible or even practical for them. In such cases, labor and management will depend upon the third-party neutral--the arbitrator--to help them resolve their dispute.

This section contains readings which will discuss the general concept of contract administration, the methods of handling a grievance, an analysis of how a grievance flows (grinds) through the process and a case example of a dispute.

11.

ADMINISTRATION OF THE UNION CONTRACT

PAUL E. HOFFNER

Having negotiated and executed a written agreement or memorandum of understanding, and following ratification by the union membership and approval by appropriate management levels, a company is now faced with the difficult task of administering the negotiated agreement for the period spelled out in the contract.

The administration of any collective bargaining agreement falls on the shoulders of management. (The union polices the agreement through the steward system and the grievance procedure). The tenor of that administration will weigh heavily on the type of relationship that develops between the parties, not only during the terms of the present agreement, but at future negotiating sessions and in future agreements.

Too often, the administration of a collective bargaining agreement is perceived as being of lesser importance than pre-negotiation planning and the actual negotiation of the agreement. Yet, it is a truism that what happens during the life of the negotiated agreement will bear on how well, or how poorly, the company accomplishes its mission through the efforts of its represented employees.

The primary step in administering the negotiated agreement is for supervisors and management of the company to know what has been agreed to between the parties, and possibly as important, what has not been agreed to. Mere reading of the words will not suffice. The company negotiating team was no doubt composed of very few people. Unless there is a single individual in the company who is ultimately responsible for the overall administration of the negotiated agreement and he/she (Personnel Director, Labor Relations Director) was also a constant part of the pre-negotiation process, the accurate administration of the agreement can be impaired even before its inception. Items that were of major consequence to the company in negotiations can be watered down or lost entirely in the faulty administration of a labor agreement. Different members of supervision and management cannot administer the words and phrases of the contract as they understand and interpret them. Rather, they must attempt to give those words and phrases the meaning and intent that the parties agreed to in negotiations.

Company-wide understanding of what the contract calls for is difficult at best, but it is an essential part of efficient and effective administration. It must be recognized that the contract cannot cover every conceivable situation that will arise during its lifetime. Like the Constitution of the United States, it must be interpreted for new and revised situations that occur regarding the working conditions of the employees covered by the agreement. As the Supreme Court of the United States interprets the U.S. Constitution, its decisions are not universally admired. Likewise, in a labor-management relationship, the parties set up a grievance procedure to resolve not only violations of actual contract provisions but applications and interpretations of the meaning of the contract. Decisions emanating from the grievance procedure will favor the company in some cases, the union in other cases, and neither party on occasion. These decisions, whether arrived at by arbitration or concession by either party, become the building blocks of contract administration. In addition, traditional practices followed by the parties and not specifically covered in the agreement form an important part of contract administration--"Past practice." It is essential to keep accurate records of all grievance settlements and arbitrator's decisions.

The possibility of third-party determination of grievance settlements focuses even more importance on the past practices between the parties. "Past practice" is defined as, and includes, management practices not covered in the agreement that have been established over a period of time, which have gone unchallenged by the union, or are followed regardless of what is stated in the contract. Past practice will be used by the union in pursuing a grievance and by the agency in defending a grievance. Where the negotiated agreement calls for arbitration, a company can be assured that the impartial arbitrator will look to past practices to try and determine the intent of the parties.

Of importance in this regard is whether the negotiated agreement is a continuing agreement that has been renewed upon expiration or whether it is the company's first contract with a particular union.

If the agreement is a continuing one, the parties have already built up in their administration of the agreement considerable "past practices" in that administration. Depending on a company's strength of administration these past practices can be helpful or harmful in the day-to-day relationship between the parties. This array of past practices can be significant as a guide to what the "words mean" and the intent of the parties. Normally when a collective bargaining agreement is renewed and the parties have not agreed to change the language in a section or article of the contract, the company would be on tenuous ground by changing the "past practice" of what was done under that section or article.

When a company and a union sign their first agreement there is less in the way of past practice to look to (except practices that operate under company rules and regulations), and the intent of the negotiators is even more important. However, in most collective bargaining agreements there is prevailing practice on the meanings of certain words and phrases. In a dispute in this area, management should look to generally accepted meanings. Of course, the company can explore the whole range of collective bargaining agreements in other activities by a particular union and the meanings given to similar words and phrases in those agreements.

The important relationship between past practices and the administration of the agreement is that the company must not allow what will become "past practices" to develop helter skelter and without the approval of appropriate management. Decisions of supervisors, management answers on grievances, management commitments to unions must be researched and thought through if management is to prevent "past practices, from developing into adverse decisions against the company in future grievances and arbitration. Generally speaking, one or two isolated incidents would not bind a company to "past practice" but, unless the company is alert in monitering its actions, these isolated incidents can become established past practices over a period of time.

Whether the negotiated agreement is a continuation of an existing one or is a new agreement with a new union, the task of efficient and effective administration of the agreement is monumental. While few negotiate the agreement, many administer it. In the company, every supervisor and manager has the authority to commit the company in the administration of the agreement. The supervisors and managers must either have the knowledge of the intent of the agreement or be able to secure that information in a timely fashion from the activity of the labor relations personnel. Since solution of employee problems or grievances at the company's lowest level is a hallmark of effective labor relations, the first-level supervisor must know how far he can go to settle a problem or resolve a grievance, without surrending in administration what the company would not surrender in negotiations.

Reprinted with permission, Center for the Study of Labor Relations, Indiana University of Pennsylvania, 1980.

12.

CONTRACT ADMINISTRATION: THE PROCESS OF RESOLVING GRIEVANCES

DONALD S. McPHERSON

Collective bargaining does not begin or end at the bargaining table. In fact, while the glamor and mystery of the process of collective bargaining are called to mind by negotiations, the heart of the process is contract administration. Much time and effort go into preparing for negotiations and bargaining a contract, but both labor and management will spend far more time living daily with the contract and developing their relationship under it.

In the most commonly accepted model of labor-management relations, the responsibility of management is to implement the collective bargaining agreement, while the responsibility of the union is to police or enforce the agreement. The mechanism through which the two parties interact in administering the contract is the grievance procedure.

The Nature of the Contract

The collective bargaining agreement, or contract, is a unique feature of the system of industrial relations which has developed in the United States since the passage of the National Labor Relations Act in 1935. At its most basic level, the contract represents a covenant between the union, representing the employees, and the employer concerning the manner in which work will be performed. More specific details of this work relationship are contained in the typical collective bargaining agreement in the United States than in any similar document in any other country in the world. In many countries, in fact, labor and management do not commonly work under a written contract. But in the United States, the trilogy of mandatory collective bargaining issues--wages, hours, and other terms and conditions of employment--covers a potentially enormous territory.

Our system of industrial relations begins with the assumption that there is a natural and legitimate divergence of interests between employers and workers concerning wages, hours, and working conditions. Collective bargaining agreements, and the process of negotiation which produces them, are not attempts to eliminate this divergence but rather to recognize it as legitimate and institutionalize methods to deal with it. The basic objective of collective bargaining is to channel the conflict so that the legitimate interests of both employer and employee are protected. The process of negotiating a contract attempts to forge an accord out of this conflice, and the written agreement symbolizes and puts into practical, operational terms the details of the accord.

Once employees have exercised their right to choose a union as their exclusive bargaining agent, the union and the employer incur a legal obligation to meet and confer in good faith with respect to wages, hours, and other terms and conditions of employment. While neither side is compelled to make or accept any specific proposal of any of these topics, both are required to bargain about them in good faith, with an intent to reach agreement. If an agreement is reached, it must be reduced to writing and signed by both parties. Such a contract is then enforceable in a court of law and each party incurs the legal obligation to insure that the contract is performed as written and intended for its duration.

In a strict sense, then, there is no such thing as a "labor contract" or a "union contract." The collective bargaining agreement is a document which legally binds both labor and management equally to its terms and conditions. Of course, someone must take the initiative to implement the agreement, and since it is the employer who pays wages, sets hours, and generally controls the employment process, it falls to management to implement the contract. But since the agreement binds both parties mutually, it falls to the union, in this process of contract administration, to enforce the correct implementation of the contract.

Rights of Union and Management

The union chosen by the employees is legally their exclusive bargaining agent. Once chose, no other representative of labor may speak or claim to speak for the workers or be heard or recognized by management. The rights which employees secure through collective bargaining are, therefore, collective, not individual, rights. Once collective bargaining begins, individuals and groups give up their rights to self-representation before the employer so that all employees in the bargaining unit can benefit from the power of a single agent's representing them. It is the union, as their agent, which is a party to the contract and not each worker as an individual. The union must enforce the agreement on behalf of all employees in the bargaining unit. Thus, while any individual worker may have a complaint about the way the contract is being administered and has the right individually to present it, management may only adjust the complaint in a manner which is consistent with the collective bargaining agreement. The union, as the exclusive representative of all the employees, may grieve management's action if it believes the contract was violated and only the union, not an individual, may take a grievance to arbitration.

Management and the union will probably have somewhat divergent views of the nature of management's rights under the collective bargaining agreement. It is generally conceded by both parties that there are certain "inherent" management rights, such as the right to make policy, to set production standards, to arrange work schedules, to adopt the budget, to structure the organization, to control the facilities, and to select and direct the work force. These rights have their foundation in the fact that management represents an employer who owns the capital which provides the physical plant, raw materials, and work opportunity in the first place. Beyond these inherent rights, management has historically held to what may be called the "reserved theory" of management rights, in which all rights not specifically conceded to or shared with the union in the bargaining agreement are reserved to management. In this view, unless a certain right is specifically stated as a union prerogative in the contract, management retains control.

But the union will most likely see the area of management rights from a somewhat different perspective. Since the equality of the parties is derived from the nature of the collective bargaining process, the union will probably subscribe to what may be labeled the "trusteeship theory" of management rights. Conceding the existence of certain inherent management rights and the responsibility of management to take the initiative in implementing the contract, the union will probably maintain that the contract itself determines which party has any other rights in their relationship. The parties thus have entirely equal, though differing, roles. Whether management or the union has a particular right, from this perspective, depends entirely upon what they actually did (or did not) negotiate and how they actually perform under their agreement. Management is not automatically assumed to retain all rights not expressly given up or shared. It is from these differing views of the nature of collective bargaining, and of management rights, which many grievances grow.

Origin of the Grievance Procedure

The collective bargaining agreement itself, and the grievance procedure in particular, represent a fundamentally important trade-off between the employer and the union as the result of negotiations. Prior to the negotiation of the contract, the workers might strike over anything they wished; even the most minor disagreement might cause a walkout. At the same time, thc employer might decide to fire the strikers and hire substitute workers, or to take the strike rather than agree to demands, or to lock out the workers. In short, any disagreement could lead to economic and industrial welfare. The trade-off which the contract represents, then, is that management agrees to a mutual determination of some working conditions in return for the union's agreement to work for a specified period of time under those conditions without striking or otherwise seeking to change the conditions. Assuming that the parties, even under a contract, will still have naturally divergent interests and differing views of management's rights, what will then be done to deal with the inevitable disagreements which will arise? And how will disagreements over contract interpretation or changes of violations be handled? The grievance procedure meets this critically important need.

The grievance procedure represents the recognized, formal mechanism through which the union can fulfill its legal obligation in contract administration: to police or enforce management's implementation of the agreement. When the union disagrees with a management action, it grieves. Similarly, because its actions are subject to formal testing in the grievance procedure, management fulfills its obligation to implement the agreement correctly.

Of course, from the union's viewpoint, it would not be satisfactory simply to be able to have a grievance heard and decided by management, for it is management itself which is probably the subject of the complaint. So the typical grievance procedure, reflecting the trade-off for a no-strike agreement, ends with a neutral third party deciding whether the union or management is correct in its interpretation: the process of binding arbitration. Arbitration is both a protection for each party and an incentive for them to work out their differences themselves without involving an arbitrator. On the one hand, each party may hold fast with its position if they are in fundamental disagreement over some issue. On the other hand, since the arbitrator is a completely objective outside party, there can be no predicting whether one will "win" or "lose" and a victory or defeat may set far-reaching precedents for the duration of the agreement. It is much in the interests of both management and the union, therefore, to work out their disputes within the grievance procedure if they possibly can do so, rather than to let them proceed to the last step, binding arbitration.

The grievance procedure potentially represents an extremely valuable tool for management and the union as they develop their relationship under the contract. It is a mechanism for channeling conflict by identifying problems quickly and clearly, rather than letting them fester or be misinterpreted. The procedure also serves as a kind of safety valve for "letting off steam" with respect to problems which, while they may not be contractual violations, nevertheless must be dealt with. If they are to be most effective and efficient in their roles, then, both management and the union should place a high priority on resolving grievances as quickly as possible. In this way, the complaining employee and the union, as well as the management, get a "day in court" with a due process procedure for investigating and hearing about the problem and the actual parties involved participate in the resolution. The ultimate objective should be a just, fair settlement of the problem consistent with the terms and conditions of the collective bargaining agreement.

Why do disagreements arise between the union and management about the meaning of the contract when both participated actively in negotiating it and should know the meaning of their agreements? Sometimes they have been unable to agree to each other's viewpoint on an issue and, in order to promote a settlement, have agreed to compromise language which does not directly address the problem which remains between them. In such instances, the parties deliberately leave the solution of the issue to the grievance procedure. Similarly, a failure to agree may lead the parties to decide to leave out language concerning a particular issue altogether, postponing deliberately the solution of the problem and leaving it for the grievance procedure.

Then, too, the parties may have agreed to language which they thought was clear but, in the cold light of reality after the bargaining, seems quite ambiguous. Or, they may simply have assigned different meaning to the same language, since they negotiate from their individual frames of reference. In either case, the grievance procedure will be relied upon to clear up the ambiguity. Finally, there are always unanticipated events or conditions which were not addressed at all in the negotiations and which seem not to be addressed at all by specific contract provisions. In these instances, too, the grievance procedure will determine the rights and prerogatives of the union and management. Both parties can thus also be assured that the grievance procedure, as it solves some problems and highlights others, will affect the next contract negotiations.

As the party responsible for policing management's implementation of the contract, the union's role in administering the agreement is primarily reactive. It responds to problems or complaints and attempts to foresee problem areas and forewarn management about incorrect interpretation of proper actions or procedures. Since it attempts to contain the resolution of all complaints within the language of the contract because it has surrendered its ultimate right to strike in exchange for the agreement, the union must always try to test the strength of the contract, to "stretch" it to cover as many issues as possible. Again, this perspective follows naturally from the union's view that the rights of both parties are grounded in the contract itself and not in some unlimited reservoir of rights which management alone controls.

The union must also use the grievance procedure as a political mechanism. As the exclusive bargaining agent, to which employees pay their dues, the union will always be subject to the time-worn question of the worker: "What have you done for me lately?" It is through the grievance procedure, by pressing its interpretation of employee rights secured in the contract, that the union attempts to give definition to, and widen if possible, the control by workers over their working conditions. It will, therefore, always be publicizing to the membership information about employee rights, about grievances won, and about situations of which employees should be wary. Some grievances may, therefore, come into the process for political reasons unrelated strictly to their merit, as judged by contract language. The union, which shares the legal responsibility for administering the contract, is also the exclusive representative of the employees and it also has the legal responsibility to serve them and represent vigorously their interests.

Just as it is natural and legitimate for the union to stretch the contract to preserve and expand its rights, management, for its part, should strive to preserve its prerogatives by defending and securing a recognition of managerial rights. Since it customarily takes the role of initiator, to which the union reacts, management will shoulder a heavy responsibility for setting the tone of the labor-management relationship. It must, therefore, take great care to implement the contract uniformly and consistently. Since every manager, every supervisor, has the authority to commit management to a particular course of action when he or she makes a decision, achieving consistency is no easy task.

If the relationship is to be a responsible and productive one, management and the union must live together under the contract in good faith, recognizing the legitimate interests and concerns of each other. Both have an interest in maintaining the strength, sophistication, and stability of the other. They must know each other's representatives and each other's goals. They may even want to consider joint training of union representatives and management supervisors so that both understand the contract, the negotiations which produced it, and the grievance procedure which will enforce it as well as their roles in the process. Management can usually expect that since the grievance procedure is such an important tool to the union, the union team responsible for grievances will be knowledgeable about the process and well trained. It must face up to the challenge of having its supervisors, especially those at the first level, equally capable and sophisticated in their knowledge of the contract and their ability to use the process to resolve grievances as quickly as possible. Education and training thus become crucial to both parties if the grievance procedure is to be used efficiently, effectively, and responsibly, which is essential for collective bargaining to work.

Elements of the Grievance Procedure

While they may vary in the number of steps or levels they contain, most grievance procedures are similar in their basic structure. Most try to combine an initial period of time during which grievances can be investigated and possibly resolved informally with later periods during which the investigation and response are very formal, with written records kept and firm positions developed. Most also stipulate very strict time limits for each stage and end with third party intervention in the form of binding arbitration. Figure 1 illustrates, in flow chart form, a model grievance procedure.

(Figure 1)

MODEL GRIEVANCE PROCEDURE

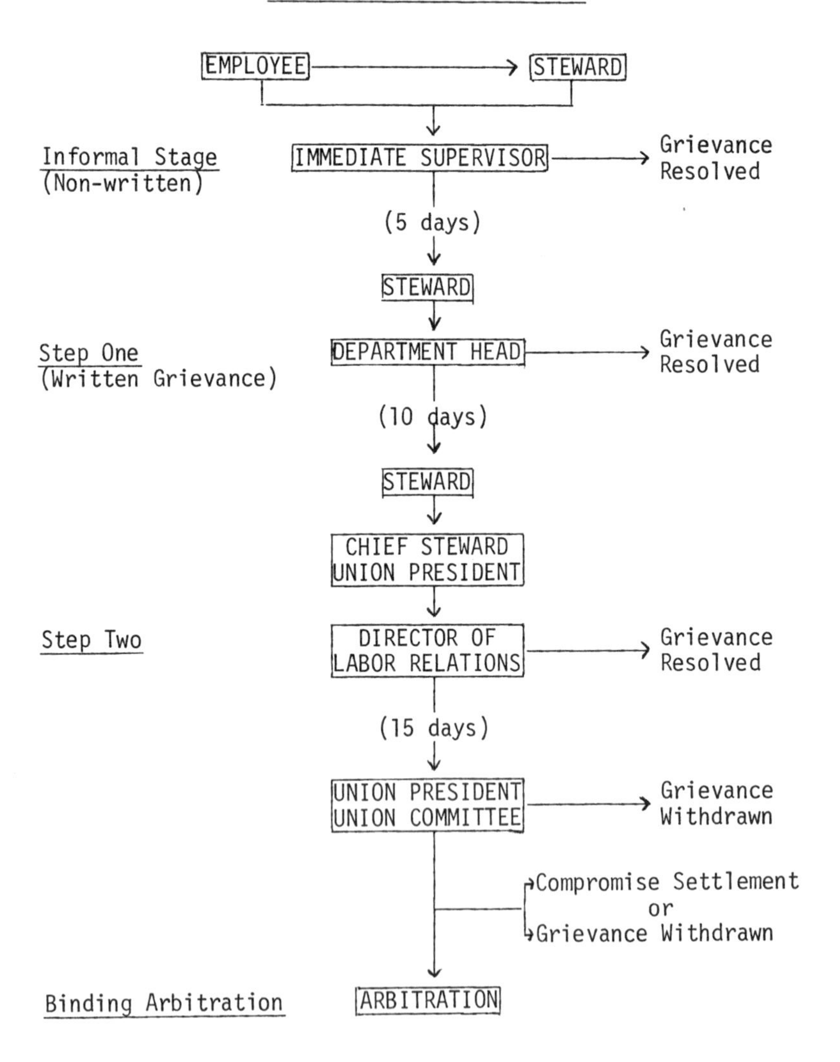

The typical grievance procedure begins with an initial, informal step. At this stage, the complaint or problem may not even yet be considered a "grievance." It is probably not written. An employee or union shop steward goes directly to the lowest management person able to solve the problem, usually the first level supervisor, and attempts to define the issue and to indicate what action will eliminate the friction. If the problem is resolved satisfactorily at that level, it does not become formally involved in the grievance procedure.

This leaves open the question of what the manager should do if approached directly by the employee with a problem in the absence of the union steward. An employee has the right to grieve without union representation. However, the union has the right to insure that any adjustment of employee grievances does not itself violate the contract, since the union alone is the representative of all members of the bargaining unit. If the problem can be handled quickly, easily, and efficiently, the supervisor may want to resolve it with the employee directly. In such a case, the union steward may not be involved or even informed, although failure at least to inform the union will probably not contribute to good relations. But if it is clear that a satisfactory, easy solution is not at hand, or if the problem impacts upon conditions covered in the collective bargaining agreement, or if it involves potential employee discipline, the manager will probably want to seek out the union steward and involve him or her from the earliest stage in the process. The steward, of course, will want to be involved since it is a central part of the steward's role to be of service to employees and to protect the interests of the union. Then, too, if no violation of the contract has occurred and the employee has an unjustified complaint, the steward's role in explaining the lack of contractual support can be an invaluable resource for the supervisor sophisticated enough to process effectively.

If the problem cannot be resolved at the informal step, it will probably become a formal grievance to be presented to management by the union steward at the next lowest level having authority to remedy the complaint. The union must now take care to investigate fully all circumstances surrounding the grievance and must commit its complaint to writing, specifying the provisions of the contract allegedly violated and the specific relief being sought. The union will be given an opportunity to argue its case and, following its own complete investigation and within a specific time frame, management must respond to the grievance in writing. If the relief sought is granted, the problem is resolved. If not, the union has the option of carrying the grievance forward to the next higher step. At each step, the union representative will investigate the case and consult with other union officials concerning the meaning of the contract, previous grievances and arbitration awards, and overall strategy. Similarly, the management representative will investigate the grievance at each step and consult with other appropriate managers concerning their view of the issue and management's response.

Frequently, the grievance procedure will involve the first level supervisor and the shop steward at step one, the department or division head and the chief steward at step two, and the director of personnel or industrial relations and the union international representative at step three. If the union is not satisfied with the response at the highest level of the employer's organization and decides to take the issue to arbitration, each party may be represented not only by the officials present for the lower steps, but also possibly by legal counsel.

At each step in the grievance process, very strict time limits are usually stipulated and enforced. Most contracts, for example, specify precisely the length of time which a grievant has to initiate the grievance process after he or she first knew, or should have known, about the incident giving rise to the complaint. Assuming that the contract has a "time of essence" clause, a failure of the union to present the grievance at each step within the timeliness limits can itself be justification for the dismissal of the grievance, regardless of its merit, by management.

In the discussion thus far, the concept of a "grievance" has been deliberately given rather loose definition. Managers and union leaders differ between and among themselves on what a grievance is, or should be. On the most restrictive end of the continuum, a grievance is an allegation that a specific provision of the collective bargaining agreement has been violated. Operating in this context, if the union is unable to cite a specific violation of explicit contract language, the grievance may be dismissed on its face as lacking merit or substance. At the other extreme, a grievance is any complaint, gripe, or problem which an employee or the union brings to the attention of management. Obviously, in this context, the exact contract language may be somewhat less central and the focus will be on resolving the problem. Clearly, even if the parties operate within the more restrictive context, complaints and problems which are not valid grievances will still arise and will still have to be resolved, even if outside the formal grievance process. But, just as clearly, the definition and understandings of the nature of a grievance which the parties arrive at during bargaining will greatly influence the workings of the grievance process, the relationship between union and management, and the role which each plays in contract administration.

There is no doubt, in any case, that an alleged violation of the terms of the collective bargaining agreement will constitute a grievance. This type of grievance may include an alleged violation of an explicit provision, or an alleged improper interpretation of a provision, or an alleged violation of the intent of the parties when they reached agreement on some provision. But a grievance might also charge a violation of law. Many contracts contain an explicit recognition of the responsibility to obey relevant laws and certainly the responsibility is present regardless of contract language. Some contracts specifically recognize the controlling influence of certain directly relevant statutes, such as those dealing with health and safety or equal employment opportunity and sometimes incorporate the language or standards of the law itself in the contract provisions. Then, too, some contracts specify that the grievance procedure will first be used when a violation of the law is to be charged, before referring the allegation to the appropriate authorities. In any such instance, the grievance procedure will be used to handle charges of legal violations and, presumably, it will be to the advantage of both management and the union to resolve the complaint in the grievance process rather than to incur the time and expense of litigation. Violations of the law also include alleged violations of the rules or procedures of regulatory or enforcement agencies charged with administering particular statutes. It must be noted, however, that the individual employee who believes his or her rights under a law have been violated maintains access to resolve the complaint not only to the grievance procedure, but also to the courts. The outcome of a grievance will not be binding upon a court, nor will a court decision preclude a grievance settlement. Since the rights are of different kinds, one grounded in citizenship and the law and the other in employment status and the collective bargaining agreement, an employee cannot be foreclosed from pursuing both channels.

In addition to charging a violation of contract language or of the law, a grievance might also allege a violation of a standard practice or procedure, whether or not it is mentioned in the collective bargaining agreement. The actual practice of the parties has long been held to be as powerful as contract language in determining their intent, or their interpretation of a provision, or their understandings of management rights. If, for example, it has been a standard practice for the employer to provide a hot lunch over several years or several contracts, the provision of a hot lunch may itself become a term and condition of employment which the employer may not unilaterally terminate even though the subject of lunch may never be mentioned in the agreement. Similarly, if the contract establishes an eight hour work day, but the practice of the employer has long been to permit quitting fifteen minutes before the end of the shift so that employees may wash-up, the wash-up time may become a "past practice" which the employer may not unilaterally eliminate under some understanding of management rights. In considering such examples, the validity of a grievance will depend entirely upon the actual conduct of the parties and the language of their contract in each specific case, but it should be clear that the ways in which management and the union act are often as important as the language they have agreed to in the contract. The potential for this type of grievance adds even more significance to the uniformity and consistency with which management implements the agreement and the vigilance and vigor with which the union polices it.

Finally, a grievance may allege a violation of accepted standards of fair treatment. Such a grievance, while more than just a "complaint", may still not be grounded in specific contract language. Yet the parties have a mutual legal obligation to perform their contract in good faith and this obligation makes arbitrary, capricious, or discriminatory application of the terms and conditions of the agreement itself a violation. While such a grievance may be more difficult to sustain in the absence of explicit contract language, examples of obviously unfair treatment may also be very difficult to explain to a neutral third party in arbitration.

Since it is the only representative of the employees which management may recognize, the union incurs a special obligation to represent the employees fairly. Over the last 30 years, the courts have gradually enunciated the nature of a "duty of fair representation" which every union undertakes even though such an obligation is nowhere mentioned specifically in collective bargaining laws. To avoid breaching its duty, the union must not use the grievance procedure in any way which is arbitrary, discriminatory, in bad faith, or negligent with respect to any member of the bargaining unit. A breach of the duty of fair representation is not only an unfair labor practice, but also grounds for a suit against the union as an organization by an employee so mistreated. For example, a union cannot refuse to process a grievance of a non-member since it is the exclusive representative of all employees in the bargaining unit regardless of their membership or non-membership in the union itself. Likewise, it certainly cannot discriminate in the processing of grievances on the basis of race or sex of an employee nor can it treat employees differently because of internal union politics. Less than complete investigations of the merits of grievances or failure to observe the contractual time limits in processing the grievance have been construed by courts as negligence and a breach of the duty. Unions are thus well advised to investigate all grievances thoroughly, to make careful merit determinations, and to process grievances diligently.

Of course, the union may agree to settle a grievance through a compromise with management, accepting some measure which is less than the relief initially sought. Here it is important to note, as party to the contract and the custodian of the grievance process, a grievance filed by the union on behalf of a member may be settled by the union regardless of the wishes of the individual employee who may have brought the grievance in the first place. Of course, if such a settlement is contrary to the terms of the collective bargaining agreement, the settlement itself may be grieved. But the point is, again, that collective bargaining rights are collective and not individual; it is the union, as the exclusive bargaining agent of all the employees in the bargaining unit, which is a legal party to the contract. It has already been noted that individuals may pursue settlement of their grievances without the presence or participation of the union. But even in those cases, the union must at least be informed of the settlement which management undertakes and the union may grieve that decision if it believes the settlement violates the collective bargaining agreement.

Sometimes, inexperienced union or management representatives may be tempted to "horsetrade" in the settlement of grievances. Management might, for example, offer to settle some grievances if the union agrees to drop others. Such horsetrading violates the law and the duty of fair representation. While a union can certainly accept a compromise settlement, such settlements should always be considered in relation to the merit of the individual grievance. Accepting a relatively weak compromise solution to a weak grievance might thus be a sound decision and well within the union's proper role; but accepting a weak solution to a highly meritorious grievance for reasons unrelated to merit will probably leave the union and potentially management open to legal challenge and liability. Management, for its part, may not be in collusion with the union in any way which interferes with its duty to fairly represent to employees or management may become co-liable for legal violations. The resolution of grievances is thus a process in which both the union and management bear heavy legal and ethical responsibilities and, therefore, a process in which the representatives of both parties must be knowledgeable and sophisticated if collective bargaining is to be productive.

While an individual employee may file a grievance and press his or her own case without union representation, only the union can take the grievance to the final step of the grievance procedure, binding arbitration. Since an arbitrator's decision of a grievance may have far reaching effects on the entire bargaining unit, the courts have declared that only the union, as the exclusive bargaining agent, may make the decision to go to arbitration. The courts have recognized that the union has institutional considerations in the development of its relationship with management which must be considered in deciding whether to press a particular grievance beyond the final management level. Furthermore, since the parties customarily divide equally the cost of arbitration, financial considerations must be given weight as the union decides which of countless grievances it may wish to pursue to a final resolution. Since the arbitrator's decision will be final and binding and will set a precedent on that issue at least for the life of the contract, the union must also consider carefully the prospects for winning and losing its case. While the prospects for winning must not be a consideration in pursuing a meritorious grievance up to arbitration, because of the duty of fair representation, the costs and benefits of a win or loss at the final step are obviously valid considerations. Thus, the courts have held that the union cannot be reasonably bound to take any particular grievance to the final, binding, and frequently expensive step of arbitration, no matter what the merits of the individual grievance. Again, at arbitration, the collective bargaining rights of employees belong to their exclusive, collective agent and not to the individuals which the agent represents. The union must constantly balance the concerns of the individual grievant and the concerns of the entire bargaining unit as it conducts itself throughout the grievance process.

Resloving Grievances: Union and Management Roles

Why should the union want to be involved in every employee complaint rather than to encourage employees to resolve problems personally with the supervisor if possible? The latter course of action might seem quite reasonable, and sometimes preferable, to the individual worker. Most people sincerely believe that "the personal touch" can make a difference in settling disputes and many employees fear that a "trouble-maker" lable might be attached to them if they file a formal grievance. Besides, it has already been noted that the individual employee does have the right to take a grievance directly to management without the intervention or assistance of the union and that management has the right to adjust the grievance directly in a manner consistent with the contract.

In the first place, it is the primary responsibility of the union's grievance representative, usually called a steward, to know the contract, relevant laws, and the rules and regulations governing working conditions. Few individual employees have the knowledge that any effective steward must have simply because the individual worker ordinarily has no need for such information. The steward's familiarity with the contract language, the history of the negotiations, and the past practices of the parties under the contract will be of invaluable assistance in formulating and presenting even a seemingly trivial complaint. Then, too, many people overestimate their own resolve in directly confronting a supervisor with a complaint. The presence of a knowledgeable, effective steward can help insure that no intimidation, actual or imagined, occurs.

Perhaps even more importantly, there are few isolated, completely individual complaints. Virtually every potential grievance involving terms and conditions of employment affects other employees individually or as a group and virtually every supervisor's response to a grievance will have implications for other employees, for the union, and for management itself. As the exclusive agent, the union depends for its strength upon collective action not only in negotiations but also in the resolution of problems which arise under the terms of the contract.

Furthermore, employees frequently misunderstand management's orientation to the filing of grievances. Of course, it is a natural tendency to want not to have complaints and frequently a lack of complaints is viewed as an indicator of good performance. But the knowledgeable, competent manager knows that working with people makes inevitable some problems and differences in judgment or opinion and a good supervisor welcomes the opportunity to settle as quickly as possible those problems which do arise. Thus, a supervisor who is trained and sophisticated in contract administration will not be threatened by the filing of a formal grievance and will have little cause for viewing such action as troublemaking. Indeed, to the contrary, the grievance procedure was established by management and the union so that an orderly, efficient, non-threatening process would be available for the identification and resolution of problems. The grievance procedure gives employees, through the union, a voice in determining their working conditions. Such a right is secure only when it is appropriately and consistently exercised.

The union, therefore, has a vested interest in participating in the resolution of grievances. Any management would react with suspicion if the union suddenly objected to a practice after having knowingly permitted it to exist for some period of time without objection. Management would rightfully question why the union didn't raise an objection at the earliest opportunity if it believed a contractual violation occurred. It is thus important for employees to take their complaints to the union in order that this process of screening and evaluating management actions and asserting the union's legitimate interest can occur.

Finally, the "track record" or grievances will affect the bargaining positions of both the union and management when the contract is renegotiated.

Each party will examine the nature of the problems which have arisen under the contract and, if necessary, will formulate new language proposals to solve these problems in the new contract. Both parties thus have an interest in keeping formal records of significant employee complaints, in developing their positions on the issues raised by those complaints, and in determining the contract language and procedures which will dispose of those issues.

Management also has highly significant vested interests in the operation of the grievance procedure. During the term of the contract, management will want to carry out in good faith its duty to implement the agreement and will also want to avoid any erosion of its own rights and prerogatives and any weakening of its bargaining position in the next negotiations. Management must, after all, be accountable for its performance and will thus take great care to maintain the authority necessary to carry out its responsibilities.

There is no doubt that management can take a certain degree of initiative in attempting to prevent problems which may rise to grievances, at least to the degree they can be anticipated. But, in the end, management must meet its responsibility to take those actions necessary to direct the enterprise within the terms and conditions of the agreement. To the union falls the duty of raising objections as it meets its duty to police the agreement.

Once a grievance does arise, management assumes the reactive role. It must not only sit in judgment on its own performance with some measure of objectivity, but also weigh its own interests in responding to the grievance. If it is possible to resolve the issue immediately, management will want to do so. In any case, there will be a substantial management interest in resolving most complaints as quickly and efficiently as possible. But, ultimately, if management believes that a fundamental issue of contract interpretation is involved and no compromise solutions are possible, it must have the resolve to maintain its position and deny the grievance. The union, then, assumes the reactive role again and must decide whether to take the issue to arbitration.

In fulfilling their mutual obligations to administer the collective bargaining agreement, management and union representatives at each level of the grievance procedure will require highly developed skills in four general areas. First, they must have a detailed knowledge of the contract and the ability to interpret and apply its language. Secondly, they must have well developed human relations skills, especially the ability to be active, intense listeners. Thirdly, the participants in the process of contract administration must have the ability to empathize: they must be able truly to see the situation from the viewpoint of the other party. Only in this way can the circumstances of a grievance really be understood and only with this ability can the representatives of each party develop strategy to respond to the arguments of the other. Finally, the representatives of both union and management must be effective advocates for their respective interests.

Investigating Grievances

While it seems relatively self-evident to say that the steward must have an expert working knowledge of the collective bargaining agreement, such ability is, in reality, highly complex and requires great diligence and creativity. "Knowing the contract" involves much more than just reading and understanding the words which have been negotiated. The effective steward must also be knowledgeable about the intentions of the parties when they negotiated the language, about alternative language which may have been proposed but was rejected, and about the meaning attributed by the parties to the language if it represents a concession or a compromise. If the steward does not have such personal knowledge of the negotiations, union officers who did participate must be consulted. The steward must also be familiar with past grievances on the same or similar issues, relevant arbitration awards, and appropriate laws and government regulations. Finally, the steward must be an expert in the employer's personnel rules and procedures and the "past practices" of management and the union with respect to the issues involved in the grievance.

Every potential grievance must be thoroughly investigated by the union. Who was involved? When? Where? What actions were taken and by whom? What was said? Were there witnesses? Is there other corroborating evidence? These and dozens of other possible questions of fact must be investigated. Further, since any two people rarely see or hear the same event in exactly the same way, conflicting evidence must be weighed in order to reconstruct the most reliable account of the circumstances leading to the grievance. If appropriate, past disciplinary or attendance records of the employee may have to be considered as well as prior conduct by any management personnel involved. By talking with other stewards, union officers, and employees, the steward investigating the grievance will have to determine whether similar circumstances are handled differently by managers or supervisors in other departments.

Probably the most crucial part of the investigation involves the grievant. The steward must interview the grievant to determine the first-hand account of the problem from the viewpoint of the person bringing the compalint. Here, especially, the steward must be a human relations expert and an active, intense listener. In addition to gathering necessary information about the grievance, the steward must gain the trust and confidence of the employee in the union's ability to handle the problem. Without committing the union to a particular course of action before the entire investigation is completed, the steward must demonstrate a sincere interest in the complaint and empathy for the employee's point of view. In fact, union officials will be effective and credible only to the degree that they have the ability to see the grievance from the point of view of the employee involved, to understand the employee's feelings, and to appreciate the stake which the employee has in the issue. Frequently, the steward will have to deal with a highly emotional, even irrational, account of an incident from the grievant. The steward must be able to look beyond the emotional response to identify the real issue. Indeed, the employee's initial complaint may be only a symptom of a much larger problem which will emerge as the real issue of the grievance.

In most grievance procedures, once the circumstances of the complaint have been investigated, the steward will present the grievance, or assist the employee in presenting it, at the first, informal step. This step usually involves the employee's immediate supervisor and the primary aim is to resolve the grievance. The informal step is potentially the final stage of the union's process of investigation, however, since it is an opportunity to find out first hand the point of view of the management supervisor. By the same token, it is also an opportunity for management, through its supervisor, to make an initial evaluation of the nature of the problem and the strength of the union's argument and feeling about the issue. Following the informal discussion, the management supervisor has a limited period of time to do an initial investigation and to make a determination which is usually communicated verbally. If the grievance has not been satisfactorily resolved, the union may file it formally.

Not all unions make decisions regarding the merits of a grievance before the formal action of filing it. Yet, it would be a mistake to assume that every union does, or any union must, file all grievances which employees bring to its attention. Workers, like any other people, are perfectly capable of misreading or misinterpreting their rights under the contract. Furthermore, while an employee is entitled to have the union enforce clear and unambiguous contract language and to interpret language which is ambiguous in a consistent fashion, an employee is not entitled to enforcement of his or her own interpretation of the meaning of "gray areas" of the contract. The many reasons for ambiguous provisions in collective gargaining agreements have already been discussed. Since the grievant was probably not present for negotiations and does not share in the union's legal obligation to present all employees in the bargaining unit, it is not unusual for misinterpretations to occur.

Of course, if an employee's grievance has any merit, the union is obligated to pursue it diligently because of the legal duty of fair representation. But if after thorough investigation the union believes the grievance lacks merit, there are substantial reasons why it may choose not to present it to management. The union obviously must be concerned with its own credibility as it exercises its responsibility to enforce the contract. A union which indiscriminately takes every employee complaint to management as a grievance risks a serious loss in credibility and detracts from the strength of its position on grievances which do have merit. If, in short, it becomes the boy who constantly cries "wolf", it should not be surprised when management decides no longer to take its cries seriously.

Nevertheless, the stage of merit review represents a difficult political problem for the union and another illustration of the balance which must be struck between collective and individual rights. The employee expects the union to which he or she pays dues to stand behind the grievance and pursue it to victory. Yet, it is entirely possible that a "victory" for an individual worker's interpretation of some section of the contract might well be a "loss" for the rights of the entire bargaining unit. The responsible union must weigh such considerations. It is not easy to tell an employee, particularly a loyal union member, that the union finds no merit in his or her grievance. But, the union must be confident that if it has done a thorough investigation and shared with the employee its findings and judgments, the employee will appreciate the sincerity and straightforwardness of the union's decision.

Finally, it must be noted that evaluating the merits of a grievance is not the same as deciding whether it is likely to be "won" or "lost." In meeting its duty of fair representation, the union must pursue a meritorious grievance even if it is absolutely convinced that management will deny the grievance. It not only has the legal obligation to represent the individual employee and the interests of the bargaining unit, but also has the need to set forth, consistently, its view of the meaning of the contract. Such consistency may be crucially important when the union argues for new contract language at the next negotiations. In order to guarantee due process, a union is well advised to develop an internal appeal process for its merit determinations.

Writing the Grievance

Assuming that the grievance was not resolved at the informal step and that the union finds it to be meritorious, it must be reduced to writing using the form agreed upon by the parties. While the precise format of grievance forms varies, the content is generally standard. After indicating the name of the grievant and any other necessary background information, the first crucial decision the union must make is to designate the date the cause of the grievance occurred or became known. This date is important because most contracts specify a strict time limit for the filing of the grievance after the grievant knew or should have known about the factors which give rise to the complaint. If a grievance arises from a particular incident, indicating the date is simple. But it will be readily apparent that much room for disagreement exists about the date, for example, a grievant "should have known" about a new management policy. It is the date a foreman informally announced that the policy was about to be issued. Or is it the date when management first posts the notice on a bulletin board? Or is it perhaps the date when management officially sends notification to the Union? Whatever the decision, the date which is chosen is of critical importance. If, for example, management contends that the grievant "should have known" about a particular policy 60 days ago under a contract which specifies a 30 day filing limit and the union filed the grievance just five days ago, management may deny the grievance because it is untimely without even examining its merits.

After settling on the date to be indicated, the union must specify the provisions of the contract which it believes have been violated. Again, a crucial decision must be made. The written grievance is a formal position paper of the union. Having once indicated specifically the violation, the union will not be able to raise other sections of the contract later; its "homework" must be done at the time of filing. The union must, therefore, take care to stipulate all provisions under which it believes it has grounds to raise objection. Often, to guarantee flexibility, the union will make a stipulation such as: "Articles V, VI, XXII, and others." In other circumstances, the union may wish to argue "the entire contract" rather than some specific section if the dispute involves the overall relationship or the fundamental intentions of the parties. How much flexibility the union has in this regard will depend largely upon the definition of a "grievance" which has been agreed to in the contract. Whatever sections of the contract the union specifies, however, it will be confined to its arguments to those provisions for the remainder of the grievance procedure.

After indicating the specific violation(s) being alleged, the union must state in writing the nature of the grievance. Again, important choices must be made. On the one hand, the union might be tempted to put forward in writing its entire argument at this point. But a more important consideration is that it will be difficult to expand the area of the union's argument beyond what is written in its statement of the grievance. It thus becomes important for the union not to write "too much" in order that its presentation of the grievance not be restricted to only the points mentioned. What the union will most likely do is summarize, completely but very concisely, the particular actions or events which caused the grievance. For example, the union might indicate: "The foreman improperly reprimanded the grievant for refusing to work overtime."

The final important decision which the union must make at the time of filing is its indication of the relief being sought if the grievance should be upheld. It is expected that the union will seek only that relief which is necessary and appropriate to correct the alleged wrong. It is legitimate for the union to seek a reversal of a management decision which it believes to have been improper and for a grievant to be "made whole" for any damage he or she may have suffered. For example, if it believes a worker was improperly paid a lower rate than required for a particular job, the union will seek payment at the higher rate for the hours worked. But the relief should do no more than re-establish equity under the agreement. It would be improper, for example, for the union to seek the dismissal of a foreman for an alleged minor procedural error.

When the union completes this section of the form and affixes the necessary signatures of the grievant and the appropriate union officials, the written grievance is filed according to the procedures agreed upon by the parties. The grievance will be considered an official statement of the union's interpretation of the relevant portions of the contract. It is reasonable to expect that the position will be consistent with any past grievances on the same issue and that in future similar circumstances the union will assert a consistent interpretation.

Presenting Grievances

Upon receipt of the grievance, the management representative will make an initial investigation to ascertain objectivly the circumstances and facts of the case. Following this investigation, a meeting will be scheduled with the union representative to review the grievance. At the meeting the steward, usually accompanied by the grievant, will present the union's position on the issues at hand. The effective steward, of course, will have thoroughly prepared the case in advance. The steward should discuss the entire presentation with the grievant, indicating at what points, if at all, the grievant will be asked to supply information or to answer questions. The steward also should anticipate management's questions and contentions in advance and prepare responses. The entire case should be carefully organized and presented from written notes.

One problem for the steward may be the reactions of the grievant, who frequently is emotionally involved in the issue. The steward presenting the union position must, at all cost, avoid arguments or differences of opinion among the union representatives during the meeting. If such differences begin to develop, the steward will call for a brief recess so that a united front can be agreed upon and presented to management. Just as "the man who acts as his own lawyer has a fool for a client", the union will probably want to avoid letting the grievant present his or her own case and will, instead, insist that the steward be the spokesperson for the union position.

The most effective presentations are those in which the union representative sticks to the point of the grievance, defines the issue and the union's contentions clearly, and seeks to narrow the differences between the union and management. At the same time, the role of the union is to seek satisfactory resolution of the grievance and the union representative presenting the grievance should maintain the union's position on the issue. The steward should make the presentation in the context of seeking a quick and complete resolution, at the lowest possible step of the grievance procedure. When the issues have been thoroughly explored and possible resolutions have been tested, the parties either agree upon an acceptable settlement or the meeting ends and the management representative issues a written response shortly thereafter.

Hearing Grievances

The way in which management's representatives behave in handling grievances may have a substantial impact on the quality of labor-management relations. If the employees are to believe in the fairness of the grievance procedure, it is essential that management's representatives review grievances thoroughly and fairly. Although the grievance meeting is not a "negotiation" session, it is a meeting between equal parties which requires good faith and may include offers and acceptance or rejection of compromises. Like his or her union counterpart, the management representative must be a human relations expert. It is important for both the grievant and the union representative to leave the meeting with the conviction that management listened with sincere interest, understood the union's contensions, avoided snap judgments, and respected the rights and the authority of the union.

Management's representatives, like their union counterparts, must also be active, intense listeners. For example, the manager must be able to set aside the rhetoric of an overly aggressive presentation in order to truly understand the real cause for the grievance. Again, just as when the steward first evaluates the employee's complaint, it may be that the grievance is only a symptom of a larger or different problem. The manager must thus attempt to empathize both with the grievant and with the union. The ability to see the issue from the point of view of the other party and to be perceived as genuinely understanding the other viewpoint again becomes crucial.

The primary objective of the grievance meeting must be to achieve an understanding of the grievance and to get all the facts. Questions must be asked deliberately and clearly to elicit equally clear and deliberate responses. The hearing officer must be careful not to be drawn into argument or to become personally involved in the issue. Another objective is to provide the grievant and the union an opportunity to "let off steam." The effective management representative will recognize this function of the hearing process and avoid any temptation to react emotionally.

Of course, the management representative cannot escape the dilemma of being both an objective participant and an advocate for management's legitimate interests. Another function of the meeting is thus for the management representative to evaluate the strength of the grievance and the degree of the union's concern. An inability to state the grievance clearly, for example, may be a reflection of bluffing or an indication of a weak case. Further, it is possible that the union is bringing what seems to be a weak grievance largely for internal political reasons. It is thus also a part of management function at the grievance review to evaluate as best it can the union's real motivation for bringing the grievance in order to help management determine a position which might successfully resolve the grievance. When the representatives are satisfied that nothing more can be learned about the grievance and that all potential alternatives for resolution have been explored, the hearing ends.

Responding to Grievances

Following the meeting, the management supervisor must thoroughly review and investigate all of the circumstances of the grievance. The basic facts must be investigated and reviewed and any inconsistencies must be resolved. All managers involved must be interviewed to find out what they did, when, where, and why. Managers in other departments may be consulted to find out how they handle similar circumstances and to evaluate the degree of management consistency. If management has been inconsistent in its own implementation of the agreement, it may be necessary to seek a compromise settlement and then to take whatever measures are necessary to insure consistency in the future.

The management supervisor will also have to check with higher levels to determine management's view of the contract, the negotiations, and of relevant previous grievances, arbitration awards, rules, procedures, practices, and laws. The natural inclination of management will of course be to support its personnel in their decisions and, assuming they have acted correctly, management should always do so. Not to give such support would create far more serious problems. But, if a representative of management has acted incorrectly, it will be most constructive for the quality of labor-management relationships for management to admit its mistake, uphold the grievance, and handle the problem of poor managerial judgment in whatever manner is most effective and appropriate.

Once the grievance has been fully investigated and management has determined its position, the management representative must respond in writing. Management's response, like the union's initial grievance, will become an official statement of its position. It is thus important that the response be accurate, thorough, and concise. Everything which must be said should be, but no more should be written than necessary. The response should be directed specifically to the grievance at hand.

First, the response should review the facts of the case. If management disagrees with the facts as presented by the union, the disagreement should be noted. Secondly, the response should identify each of the union's contentions and provide management's response. If management agrees that the contract was violated, it should so indicate. If, on the other hand, it believes there was no violation, it should reject the union's contentions and provide the rationale for management's view of the contract. If it finds no contractual violations, the management response should clearly deny the grievance. If violations are recognized, however, the response should either explicitly grant the relief sought by the union or, if management believes from its discussions with the union that an alternative settlement will be accepted, the response should specify the relief offered. In evaluating whether or not to grant the relief sought, management must always keep in mind that ultimately the union may decide to take the grievance to arbitration. Management must thus evaluate how secure how it feels in its view of the contract in determining whether or not it can "afford" any particular grievance settlement. Of course, if management believes the union has a credible, but not strong case, it should attempt to find a settlement which will be responsive to the union's concerns without undercutting management's ultimate rights.

Higher Steps in the Procedure

At each stage, the union must evaluate management's response to the grievance. If the grievance was rejected outright, the union must decide whether to accept the rejection or to push the grievance to the next highest management level. As higher levels in the process become involved, the union will involve more of its resources--first, the local chief steward and later representatives of the international and perhaps even legal counsel. Management, likewise, must evaluate at each stage the performance of its representatives at the lower levels and the overall management interest in resolving the grievance rather than risking arbitration. If fundamental issues are involved, management will no doubt want to stand firm. But there also may be a point at which achieving a settlement of the grievance is preferable to risking the loss of a wider issue at arbitration because of the precedent which will be set with the arbitrator's award. At each stage in the process, then, the judgment and actions of the representatives of each party may lead either to a resolution or a protraction of the dispute.

Considering Arbitration

The union must also evaluate a rejection or settlement offer at each stage against the final prospect of arbitration. It must review carefully its contentions and decide, as objectively as possible, if it believes its view of the contract is correct. Since at least half the cost of arbitration is generally borne by the union, it also must decide whether it can afford to arbitrate a particular case. Such a decision must be based not only on the absolute cost, but also on whether, all things considered, the issue is sufficiently important to commit the necessary time, energy, and money.

Most importantly, the union must evaluate its chances for winning and the effects of losing. It may be that winning a particular grievance at arbitration would establish a relatively unimportant principle, while losing it may undercut a whole line of separate, but related grievances.

Finally, the union must evaluate the kinds of settlements which may be possible. Settlements which are acceptable to both parties, though they may not completely satisfy both, avoid the precedent which will be set by an arbitrator's award. Indeed, they may stipulate that a settlement is limited to a particular issue and has no impact whatever on future grievances. In addition to disposing of a grievance without going to the time and expense of arbitration, the experience of fashioning acceptable settlements can greatly contribute to the quality of the labor-management relationship. There can be little doubt the practice in finding mutually acceptable grievance settlements makes the process of achieving satisfactory resolutions in the future easier. Each party must take the risk of accepting and "selling" to its constiuency a less than entirely satisfactory settlement, with the result that a degree of mutual trust is built not only in the integrity of the other party but also in the effectiveness of the process.

It is through the grievance procedure, then, that the union and management will create the relationship within which they will work under the contract. A cooperative, productive, and mutually beneficial relationship requires all the diligence, vigilance, creativity, and good faith which the parties can bring to the process.

Reprinted with permission, Center for the Study of Labor Relations, Indiana University of Pennsylvania, 1980.

13.

GRIEVANCE CASE:

DEMIS PHARMACUETICAL COMPANY

PAUL E. HOFFNER

The following case attempts to present some of the many problems associated with the administration of a union contract, especially when the union has exercised its right to challenge management's decisions through the filing of a grievance. Following the text of the case is an example of the grievance that was filed, along with the possible management responses. It should be understood that good contract administration requires managing the workforce within the intended meaning of the union contract, and that in most cases where problems arise, closer attention to the contract language plus an appreciation for the prevention of misunderstandings can lead to the minimization of problems such as presented here.

DEMIS PHARMACEUTICAL COMPANY

CASE

On a Tuesday afternoon during the spring busy season, Robert Jones, general production foreman of Demis' main plant, received his production quotas for the subsequent two weeks. Since the production of sodium nitrate in Building 10 was being increased substantially, Jones had requested five additional people who held the job-classification title of "chemical operator." Jones sought assistance from the personnel department to select people for these jobs who had previous experience in producing sodium nitrate. Among the people assigned to Jones for the sodium nitrate production was Homer Evand, twenty-six years old, a chemical operator with nine years' experience at Demis.

On Thursday, Evand received a copy of the

posted working schedule for the next week. The schedule indicated that he was to report to building 10 the following Monday morning to work on the sodium-nitrate process. About 3:30 that afternoon, Evand walked into Robert Jones' office:

Evand: Why didn't you pick on someone else to work on sodium-nitrate? I want to remain on my present job. I was transferred to Building 20 only a few weeks ago. I've just gotten to the point where I understand my new job. Now you are taking me away and putting me back on this job.

Jones: In other words, Homer, you feel that I am imposing on you by requesting your transfer?

Evand: I am beginning to believe that you bosses are damn inconsiderate around here. Do you realize that I have been moved four times in the past five months? I haven't been able to learn any of these jobs well. Just as I get to the point where I'm beginning to be able to do the work, one of you guys hauls me off to a different department.

Does everyone get moved around as much as I, or is there something wrong with me? Am I doing such a poor job that all my bosses are trying to get rid of me?

Jones: Remember, Homer, I did request that you be assigned to my department. And you do have the job title of "chemical operator," which means that we can use you as the demands of our business dictate, so long as you work in jobs that are basically similar in nature. We've always done it this way. You've had prior experience in the sodium-nitrate production process, and I felt we needed people like you to get over the spot we're in now.

Evand: Can't you fellows plan your work? This is a poor way to run a department. No one shows any consideration for chemical operators. We get moved around like men on a checkerboard. And don't tell me that it's done fairly. No one asks us what we want to do.

Jones: I am sorry to learn that you feel this way about my department. I always thought that we clicked it off in a good manner.

Evand: Tell me, how long will I be here? Can I count on staying in this department from now on? Or am I going back to building 20 next week?

Jones: I can't promise that you will stay here. All I know is that we need production in sodium-nitrate for at least the next two weeks. I don't know what will happen after that.

Evand: I think I am getting a raw deal here. I'm going to see my union steward to file a grievance.

Homer Evand had worked in Building 20 for five weeks before being transferred back to building 10, his former department. He had an excellent work record; in fact, most of his supervisors had given him a top rating on his semiannual employee evaluations. In recent months, however, several foreman had commented that his previous enthusiasm and spirit on the job had diminished somewhat.

Two days following his conversation with Evand, Robert Jones received a written grievance from the union steward that protested the "indiscriminate transferring of chemical operators from job to job in violation of the contract." In studying Evand's grievance, Jones reviewed the union contract sections governing job transfers in the plant. The most pertinent clauses read as follows:

SECTION 1: MANAGEMENT RIGHTS

(a) Cooperation between parties and the observance of the contract is the basis of all enduring agreements. The parties to this agreement recognize that stability in wages, working conditions, production, and competency and efficiency of workers are essential to the best interests of both employees and management and agree to strive to eliminate all factors that tend toward unstablizing such conditions. It is understood that the administration and operation of the plant including but not limited to the assignment, transfer, and disciplining of workers and the establishment of production-control procedures is the responsibility of Management. . .

SECTION 21: TRANSFERS

The transferring of employees is the sole responsibility of Management subject to the following. . .

(b) It is the policy of Management to cooperate in every practical way with employees who desire transfers to new positions or vacancies in their department. Accordingly, such employees who make application to their foreman or the personnel department stating their desires, qualifications, and experience will be given preference for openings in their department provided they are capable of doing the job. . .

Jones pondered what his reply to the grievance should be and what course of action he should take.

Council 39
American Union Associates
GRIEVANCE FORM

Grievant: H. Evand

Grievant's Title: Chemical Operator

VIOLATION

Article & Section(s): Section 1, part (a). Section 21, part (b).

STATEMENT OF HOW MANAGEMENT'S ACTION OR INACTION CONSTITUTES A VIOLATION OF THE CONTRACT

Statement:

Management's decision to assign me to a new department beginning 11/13/78, when considered in addition to at least two previous assignments in the previous few months, constitutes a blatant disregard for stability in working conditions as they relate to the desires and efficiency of its employees, and therefore are a violation of Section 1, part (a) of the collective bargaining agreement.

In addition, management has a responsibility and contractural obligation to take into account the desire of the employee in making any or all work reassignments, and failure to do so, as it appears in this instance, constitutes a violation of Section 21, part (b) of the collective bargaining agreement.

REMEDY SOUGHT

Remedy:

That H. Evand be reassigned back to his previous department and that all future reassignments of work are implemented only after management has consulted with the union to insure contractural conformity.

Example of Grievance Response - Grievance Denied

August 1, 1980

SUBJECT: Howard Evand, Chemical Operator

TO: American Union Associates and Howard Evand

FROM: R. Jones, Foreman
Demis Pharmacuetical Company

The grievance alleges a violation of Sections 1 (a) and 21 (b) of the collective bargaining agreement.

While a need for employee efficiency Section 1 (a) is of great concern to the parties, a two-week assignment in the "silver nitrate" function is not viewed as having any significant negative impact on the grievant. His prior experience in this area is of significant importance for the efficiency of the production procedure in question.

Section 21 (b) is clearly intended as a "before the fact" opportunity for employees to alert management as to where they prefer to work and is not intended to require prior consultation before any transfer is directed by management.

The remedy sought by virtue of Mr. Evand's reassignment is denied.

The remedy sought by virtue of prior consultation with the union is denied.

bg

Example of Grievance Response - Grievance Acceptance

TO: H. Evand, American Union Associates

FROM: R. Jones, Foreman
Demis Pharmacuetical Company

DATE: 8-1-80

RE: Resolution of grievance filed 7-26-80

This is to confirm the agreement reached at our meeting of 7-31-80 that the grievant will be allowed to remain in his present work assignment and that all future work assignments will be made from a rotation list of chemical operators based upon seniority in the plant.

The above action will constitute a resolution of the grievance without prejudice or precedent to management's future actions.

V

EMPLOYEE DISCIPLINE

If you were suddenly approached and asked to define the word "discipline" in all probability you would associate it with punishment. This is not surprising, for discipline, in its narrowest context, is the definition of the act of imposing penalties for incorrect behavior. A broader definition would view it as including any conditioning of future behavior by the application of either rewards or penalties. This latter usage would include positive motivation, such as praise, incentive pay and participation as well as negative techniques such as reprimand, suspension and fines.

The most common definition is that of penalty utilization that inhibits or eliminates undesired behavior. Thus we will be exploring negative motivational efforts.

Clearly, the vast majority of employees do conform to regulations, policies and orders. There is a minority, however, that seem to require the stimulus brought about by penalties. In viewing their supervisory hierarchy, employees do not want either "one of the group" or an autocratic approach. They desire fair and equitable enforcement of reasonable rules and regulations.

There are two basic elements perceivable in any effective disciplinary process. The first is that discipline should be a line responsibility. Though the trend has recently been somewhat away from this, it is recognized that the impact of discipline is more effective (positive?) when taken by the line supervisor. The second element is a clear understanding of what is expected of each employee in the way of behavior. This places on management the burden of establishing reasonable rules and regulations which contribute to effective operation and not simply as a basis for punishment. The most common areas for work rules are: attendance, safety, insubordination, work hours, theft, intoxication, fighting, solicitations and dishonesty. A basic problem is assuring that employees are aware of the rules and in some cases the reason(s) for them. Many should be apparent, but it is incumbent upon management to be certain that those peculiar to its concern are covered in an orientation effort. It is also essential that the rules be enforced, both consistently and fairly. If a rule has been ignored, employees should be notified that it is now going to be enforced.

In spite of management's best efforts to have reasonable rules and to communicate them, employees situations may arise in which the facts and rules indicate the need for the application of a penalty. Supervision must then choose from among the following negative actions:

Oral Reprimand	Suspension
Written Reprimand	Demotion
Loss of Privileges	Discharge
Fines/Reductions in Pay	

The key here is to select a "penalty that fits the crime: while at the same time leads (if possible) to correction of the offending behavior.

The following statements should also serve as guides to enable supervision to maximize the effect of the corrective nature of negative discipline while at the same time permitting a reasonable maintenance of self-image for the employee being disciplined:

Actions should be done in private.
The application of discipline should carry with it a constructive element.
Actions should be taken, where possible, by the immediate supervisor.
Punishment delayed is simply punishment.
Consistency in discipline is highly essential.

A supervisor should not be disciplined in front of his/her subordinates.

Once discipline is taken, resume a normal attitude toward the employee.

When management is dissatisfied with the behavior of an employee, the above elements and guides should enable it to more effectively alter the individual's behavior so that it is more consistent with organizational requirements. The following material will expand upon the positive nature and effectiveness of discipline. The case example will not only explore a real situation, but will give some useful guidance as to how to reduce discipline to a written format.

14.

EMPLOYEE DISCIPLINE: TURNING A NEGATIVE INTO A POSITIVE

ROBERT L. GAYLOR

The establishment of a satisfactory disciplinary policy is essential if management is to carry out its primary function, the direction of the workforce. It is to the advantage of the employees as well as management that there be effective discipline and adherence to reasonable organizational rules. The smooth and efficient operation of an organization of any degree of complexity is in large part a function of the understanding and acceptance by its employees of some parameters within which they are to perform their work assignments.

In most people's minds, the word "discipline" carries with it a rather negative connotation. Typically, it is equated with the concept of punishment. Discipline can, however, be viewed from another perspective. More modernistic managerial systems are tending to shift the emphasis from the punitive aspects of discipline to its possibilities as a vital component in efforts to establish a more positive, constructive employment atmosphere. Any form of group effort, if it is to be performed efficiently, requires control, cooperation, and discipline of and by those engaged in the activity. Modern concepts of "discipline" involve its use as an instrument to not only <u>dis</u>courage activities which disrupt the group process, but also <u>en</u>courage cooperative efforts. Effective discipline can be a means of assisting workers in carrying out their responsibilities.

Generally, rules whose rationale and purpose are understood by the employees will be easier to accept and follow. More importantly, by offering some sound basis for its actions rather than simply imposing extensive regulations without explanation, management demonstrates to its employees that it recognizes and values their perceptions and reactions. This approach will serve to build an atmosphere in which the individual worker is afforded the opportunity to carry out his or her work functions, and also to derive personal satisfaction from accomplishments in the workplace.

Self-Discipline

"Discipline" can also refer to the concept of self-imposed regulation or restraint. This type of control, which originates internally, is an equally significant factor in the individual's adaptation to the demands of the work situation.

A central realization for the manager is that his or her own exemplary behavior in the area of self-discipline is prerequesite to its acceptance by employees as a method of regulating their own conduct; employees cannot be expected to practice self-discipline if such discipline is not evident within the managerial structure. Proper conduct mindful of the needs of the organization will involve compliance by supervisors and other managers with the same rules which employees must follow; managers and supervisors must be expected to obey safety rules, to be at work on time, and to dress and behave in a manner consistent with the requirements of their roles. Managers who are not prepared to establish, by their own example, proper self-discipline should not expect a demonstration of that characteristic by employees.

This approach to discipline centers around several key assumptions regarding basic tendencies of workers; that is, that the employee is "by nature" inclined to: (1) do what needs to be done; (2) carry his or her fair share of the work; and (3) operate within the social and moral limits of the work environment. The transformation of the "negatives normally associated with discipline into "positives" is based on the premise that most employees want to do the right thing. Employees generally understand that instructions and fair rules of conduct must be followed, and accept them as normal responsibilities that come with employment. Most employees will perform their work assignments, will come to work on time, will refrain from fighting, drinking or stealing at work--that is, will generally follow the supervisor's orders and live within the constraints the workplace imposes on them.

These expectations are most likely to be fulfilled when reasonable standards of conduct have been established, the employees have been informed of the standards, and the standards are enforced in an intelligent and equitable manner. When management establishes and maintains such conditions, it is more likely that employees will exhibit self-discipline (which is a manifestation of a good morale situation) and will, as a group, assist in enforcing the standards by applying social pressures to members of the workforce who deviate from them. When employees believe that management has not fulfilled its responsibilities to its employees in these areas, employee self-discipline will often break down.

That there is, at times, a need for implementation of a disciplinary mechanism does not in itself refute the above assumptions regarding the nature of the worker. Simply as a function of statistical probabilities, there will inevitably be present a small faction of disruptive individuals; it is important for the manager to realize that these workers are the exceptions to the norm, rather than the standards by which it is established.

Types of Discipline

Disciplinary methods can be categorized as either positive, intended to motivate some desired behavior, or negative, with the purpose of restraining or eliminating some behavior. Regardless of the type of discipline utilized, its purpose is to motivate the employee or employee group to observe the policies, rules, procedures and regulations that have been established to provide for the attainment of organizational objectives. Positive discipline permits employees greater freedom of self-expression and greater latitude in self-regulation. Emotionally, it generates a state of satisfaction rather than conflict and provides an atmosphere of coordination and cooperation with minimal expressions of formal authority. It is most effectively used when organizational objectives and mechanisms are understood and accepted by the employees.

One "old saw" of discipline is that "the best way to deal with problem workers is not to hire them in the first place." This is an example of the preventive method of positive discipline. An understanding of the work to be performed will enable the manager to recognize those factors in an individual's background which, although not necessarily work related, might lead to problems. Employees already on the payroll warrant management attention as well. Any manifestation of apparent psychological problems--on or off the job--must be recognized. Daily or routine performance at a skill level noticeably different from that which was apparent prior to hiring may be symptomatic of such a problem. It is also a possibility that on occasion, management may find the supervisor to be a contributing factor to a disciplinary problem.

The concept of negative discipline involves the utilization of various extrenal and usually disagreeable influences for behavior patterning. Its possibilities for success are greatest only if and when more positive methods have proven ineffective. The key weakness of this method is the possibility that external controls may only alter the individual's behavior while underlying mental and emotional problems persist.

Since individuals and the influences which affect them differ markedly, no single disciplinary approach can be appropriate under all circumstances; the manager must be prepared to vary the degree and style of discipline with the individual and the situation.

The Role of the Supervisor

Supervisors and managers must enforce the rules of an organization. This is normally achieved without imposing unnatural external controls. When such action is necessary, however, it is essential that the supervisor use sound judgment in the exercise of disciplinary power if the net effect is to be positive and constructive. The supervisor should approach a disciplinary situation with an awareness of the legalistic and procedural implications as well as an understanding of the "human nature" component involved in both the infraction and the resultant corrective action. The factors contributing to an employee's inappropriate behavior are at least as important as the act itself. Any attempt to alter behavior and prevent a recurrence of some undesirable conduct requires an understanding of the underlying causes of the behavior exhibited.

Since supervisors are only human too, it is sometimes difficult for them to maintain an objective attitude toward unacceptable employee behavior; but if they utilize a problem-solving, rather than punitive or hostile approach, they are more likely to assume a psychological posture conducive to resolution of the difficulty.

In attempting to arrive at an explanation for an employee's unacceptable behavior, the supervisor should allow for the possibility that the employee may not have been aware that a rule existed covering the conduct, or that he or she may not have known of its application in the particular situation. Certainly, employees may at times conveniently plead ignorance of a regulation after the fact; it is up to the supervisor to determine in such instances whether or not the employee was given a careful and thorough indoctrination to company rules and regulations. The supervisor may, in the case of certain extremely serious infractions, find that an assessment of the employee's physical and/or emotional fitness to perform his or her assignments in accordance with existing work rules will have to be made.

Disciplinary Action

It is imperative to the effectuation of a workable disciplinary process that responsibility for administration of disciplinary actions be established. To be effective, discipline should be a line responsibility. While staff operations, such as the personnel office, can and should provide advice, the discipline of employees is so central an element of leadership that it should reside within the supervisory chain.

The good supervisor will usually have little occasion to engage in disciplinary action. However, when it becomes necessary, the supervisor should be prepared to move forward with the unpleasant task with which he or she is confronted.

INVESTIGATE. Before taking any action, the supervisor should make every effort to ascertain exactly what happened and why. If possible, the supervisor should interview the employee to afford the latter the opportunity to present his or her account of the situation; in addition, the interview will give the supervisor the chance to make an assessment of how and whether the employee's attitude, demeanor, character, etc. may have affected his or her behavior. At this point, the supervisor must be careful not to permit subjective, emotional considerations to cloud his or her judgment in examining the situation. That is, disciplinary actions must be based on sound judgment and calculated, objective evaluations rather than on affective reactions.

The supervisor should examine the employee's personnel file. Contained therein should be information concerning behavioral situations which may have previously led to disciplinary actions; the file should contain accounts of oral reprimands, copies of written reprimands, and copies of notifications of suspension or discharge if such actions had been taken in the past. Documentation of this type will prove invaluable should the necessity arise at some future time to refute charges that the employee was not adequately warned of the consequences of his or her behavior.

The old joke about the word "assume" is certainly true in the area of employee discipline; making suppositions--especially of an accusatory nature--can be a very dangerous course of action. Before management can expect cooperation in obtaining answers to discipline-related questions, it must demonstrate to the employees and their representatives that it is investigating each and every potential disciplinary situation with an open mind. The demonstration of any other approach to such an investigation would virtually guarantee resistance by employees to management efforts.

PROGRESSIVE DISCIPLINE. It would be misleading and inaccurate to suggest that a particular disciplinary action does or ought to automatically follow as the management response to a particular type of unacceptable behavior by employees. The disciplinary action appropriate in any given situation will depend for the most part upon the circumstances of that individual situation. The common concept of "progressive discipline" is the accepted norm for disciplinary practices today. This concept provides for increasing severity of penalties assessed for behavior which is repetitive in nature. E. B. Flippo, in his book Principles of Personnel Management[1] enumerates the following types of penalties available to management:

1. Oral Reprimand
2. Written Reprimand
3. Loss of Privileges
4. Fines
5. Layoff
6. Demotion
7. Discharge

Flippo lists the penalties in order of their severity, from mild to most severe. The oral reprimand or informal talk is usually utilized for relatively minor situations. These are infractions which do little harm or result in few significant consequences when viewed isolatedly. Persistence, however, in the performance of even minor infractions may indicate a more serious problem. Usually a frank discussion between the supervisor and the employee will be sufficient to elicit the desired behavior patterns. If an initial discussion of this type is not sufficient to bring about the desired behavior alterations, it may then be necessary for the oral discussion to become more formal; it should, at this point, be noted as an official reprimand by the supervisor in his or her discussion with the employee. Of paramount importance is the supervisor's explanation to the employee of the consequences of repeating the unacceptable behavior. If carried out skillfully, this method of disciplinary activity will solve the vast majority of potential problem situations.

When the oral reprimand has failed to solve the problem, the repetition of unacceptable behavior should lead to a written warning or reprimand. This is clearly a permanent and formal action on the part of management with the employee. Such written records are particularly important in a unionized situation so that management can show the efforts it has taken to correct an employee's behavior short of deprivation of either privileges or finances to the employee. The reprimand should: state the nature of the unacceptable behavior; review any history of prior warning or discussion with the employee; cite the rules violated or other reason for which the behavior is unacceptable; outline the consequences of continued unacceptable behavior; and indicate that the employee has the right of appeal either through the employer's work rules or the established grievance procedure in a collective bargaining agreement.

Privileges can be denied an employee for unacceptable behavior in a number of ways. As an example, many employers permit employees to utilize sick leave without verification from a physician that they have been ill, except in extended periods; in situations where the employer has reason to believe that an individual is abusing sick leave, the individual may be required to provide a doctor's statement for each instance of illness. Thus, deprivation of the privilege (not being required to account for sick leave time) is tied directly to the nature of the unacceptable behavior (suspected abuse of sick leave) exhibited by the employee. Fines are also usually tied to the nature of the unacceptable behavior. For example, individuals who are tardy for work or engage in non-productive activities may be "fined" for the amount of time involved. This "docking" of pay is extremely common in the area of tardiness.

Disciplinary layoffs or suspensions are utilized for major violations or repetitions of minor infractions. Most suspensions cover reasonably short periods of time; however, it is not uncommon for an employee to be suspended for periods of more than a week in significant, but non-terminable situations. Tied into the concept of progressive discipline is a progression through the amount of suspension time an employee may have to serve for repetition of uancceptable behavior for which the individual has already been suspended at least once. This author normally uses a one-day, three-day, five-day, and then a more severe discipline approach. There is no ideal numerical structure. The desirability of a two-day suspension over one-day for a first offense, which is serious enough to warrant suspension, will be a function of the interplay of the variables discussed earlier.

Like all disciplinary actions which start at the level of written reprimands, a "notice of suspension" should be accomplished in writing with the same basic format as that outlined for the written reprimand. It is not uncommon for management to avoid the utilization of the disciplinary suspension because of its negative impact on productivity. Nevertheless, disciplinary suspension is a very common form of addressing major violations and repeated minor infractions.

Lowering an employee's salary and work level through a demotion is, of late, viewed as a less and less viable disciplinary tool. The loss of salary and status over an extended period of time often creates an intolerable working situation which causes the employee to resign or to become dysfunctional. This dissatisfaction can be contagious in group situations.

The industrial form of "capital punishment"--discharge--is the most severe type of discipline. Discharge is usually utilized for intolerable offenses of such a drastic or illegal nature that no viable alternative is apparent. This could involve a serious first-time offense such as stealing or it could be invoked as a result of the constant repetition of a lesser infraction such as tardiness. The excision of an employee from the work place is often a painful step. Like any cutting process, it leaves scars on the structure that remains. Removal of an employee also generates a situation in which it is extremely difficult for him or her to find subsequent employment in the same field. In addition to the price exacted through the trauma of such an effort is the cost for the employer in economic terms of finding and hiring a new employee to replace the individual removed.

Since discharge is such a severe penalty, it is not unusual for organizations to remove from the supervisor the right of outright discharge. Some review either by higher line or staff management is usually required prior to actually removing an employee from the payroll.

A final dimension of the concept of progressive discipline is the issue of timeliness. Discipline, to be effective, must be taken in a relatively short period of time. Discipline delayed is simply punishment.

In addition, there needs to be an understanding that the disciplinary action is not something that lasts forever except in the most severe forms. Oral and written reprimands should not be held against an employee forever. Minor offenses, if not repeated within a six, nine, or twelve month period, should be forgotten. In more severe situations, such as threatening a manager or supervisor, a much longer period of time would be considered appropriate for retaining the documentation of a disciplinary situation.

Conclusion

In a 1951 book by Richard Lester entitled Labor and Industrial Relations: A General Analysis[2], little time was spent in discussing the subject of discipline. The only references to discipline were a rather cursory examination of the impact of discharge and a short discourse on the right of unions and employees to grieve the actions of management in this area. The relative simplicity and straightforwardness of the concept at that time created little need for elaboration on it. In the years since Mr. Lester briefly addressed the concept of discipline, the rights of employees, unions, and managers have been more clearly defined through the arbitration and unfair labor practice mechanisms. Today the area of discipline is a specialty in personnel and employee relations and not simply an annoying problem to be handled with relative unconcern. Discipline clearly is an unpleasant subject not only for those being disciplined, but also for those who must effect the disciplinary action. It is, however, a concept that can carry with it the foundation for a harmonious working environment through which the organization can reach its stated goals with a minimum of disruption. A disciplinary system based upon an understanding of the employees' need to obtain satisfaction and self-actualization within the working place, and which at the same time recognizes the basic willingness of employees to be productive and provide a fair return for the salaries given to them can provide the opportunity to take a negatively perceived methodology and use it to produce positive results. Discipline is not simply punishment; nor is it "getting even." Discipline that is aimed at restructuring unacceptable behavior while at the same time maintaining the integrity of the individual is highly compatible with the organizational realities facing managers today.

FOOTNOTES

[1]Flippo, Edwin B., Principles of Personnel Management, McGraw-Hill, Inc., New York, 1976, pp. 439-440.

[2]Lester, Richard A., Labor and Industrial Relations, MacMillan, New York, 1951, p. 163.

15.

DISCIPLINE CASE:

LUNCHTIME FOR SAM JOHNSON

PAUL E. HOFFNER

The following case attempts to present some of the difficulties associated with situations that may lead to the discipline of an employee. Although solving the problem which caused the need for the discipline should be the manager's first concern, he/she must also recognize the importance of correctly expressing the disciplinary measures when the situation does warrant action. Following the text of the case are presented two examples of disciplinary letters issued to the employee. The key element here is to recognize the value in being specific and firm, yet fair in administering the disciplinary notice. This is important not only to ensure the employee's understanding of the action, but also to provide an adequate record of the events/actions taken should an additional need for discipline arise in the future.

ICEBOX COMPANY

CASE

Sam Johnson was employed by Icebox Company on 1/22/76 and had a good work record until August, 1979.

On 8/16/79, Sam and three other employees had left the plant for lunch. While two of the employees went into the eating establishment to purchase lunch, Sam and another employee remained in the automobile. Sam lit up a hand-rolled cigarette, the content of which is in dispute. Within a few minutes several plainclothes police officers descended on the car and arrested Sam and eventually the three others.

After interrogating the four employees at the police station, the officers allowed the other three to go home. Sam was held for bond because of previous convictions. The next morning he was arraigned before a judge and offered to plead guilty to a charge of possession and use of marijuana. After a discussion, Sam pleaded guilty to possession of marijuana for his own use, and received a three-month suspended one-year sentence and was ordered to pay $19 in court costs.

Sam had phoned the company from the police station to report that he would not be able to complete his shift. The company was therefore aware what had happened, and also had a meeting with the three other people who were arrested. When Sam arrived for work on his regular shift on the 17th of August, he received a letter of suspension for the violation of a company rule which read as follows:

Employee Use of Alcohol or Unlawful Drugs:

Any employees found to be in the possession or use of alcohol or unlawful drugs during working hours or on company premises or arrested for the same during non-work time shall be subject to disciplinary action at the discretion of management.

The company assumed that the grievant's plea of guilty was tantamount to an admission that he possessed marijuana and therefore refused to permit him to return to work. The grievant told the management that the substance he was smoking in the car was Fiord, "a mild, cool, smoking mixture with African Yohimbe bark." When asked why he would plead guilty to a charge of possession, he responded that he copped a plea, "because he did not have the money necessary to post bail and this was the easiest way to stay out of jail." Management then offered to reinstate him if he could prove that he was not smoking marijuana.

Sam asked a detective at the Narcotics Department to call the company. In a memo dated on the date of the call, the employer relations manager notes that the detective said he was 100% certain that the substance confiscated by the police was marijuana even though the "final lab tests were not in." When Sam did not produce any evidence that the substance was not marijuana, the company discharged him on 8/25/79. Sam appealed his discharge and asked that he be reinstated and awarded full back pay and full seniority.

Following a number of meetings regarding the discipline, management renewed its offer in a letter from the union business agent, dated September 23, 1979. The company repeated this offer at the arbitration.

Excerpts from the collective bargaining agreement:

ARTICLE IV: MANAGEMENT RIGHTS

The company shall have the right to make reasonable work rules which are designed to aid in the effective management of the organization and protect the health, safety and welfare of the employees. The company may not change an existing work rule without first consulting with the union. All work rules must be communicated to all employees. Failure to comply with company work rules shall constitute grounds for disciplinary action. Both the work rule and the disciplinary action are subject to the grievance process.

ARTICLE XI: DISCIPLINE - SECTION 4. TERMINATION

The company shall have the right to terminate the employment of any individual for just cause. Just cause shall include but not be limited to subordination, failure to perform work as assigned or failure to observe company work rules.

Example of an "Unacceptable" Disciplinary
Letter to Sam Johnson

Supervisor Brown
Icebox Company
August 17, 1979

Dear Sam Johnson:

Your behavior of August 16, 1979 was in direct violation of a company rule. As such, you are hereby placed on a two-day suspension.

Future unacceptable behavior will result in more discipline.

Regretfully,

B. Brown

Supervisor Brown

cc: Personnel File
Union Steward

Discipline Case - Exhibit 1

Example of "Acceptable" Disciplinary
Letter to Sam Johnson

Supervisor Brown
Icebox Company
August 17, 1979

Dear Sam Johnson:

This is to inform you that this letter constitutes notice of an official two-day suspension for your behavior of August 16, 1979.

Your apprehension and arrest for "possession of an unlawful drug (marijuana)" on August 16, 1979, at the Brown Derby Restaurant during your lunch break was in direct violation of the company work rule (Section II A of Employee Handbook) stating:

"Any employees found to be in the possession or use of alcohol or unlawful drugs during working hours or on company premises or arrested for the same during non-work time shall be subject to disciplinary action at the discretion of management."

You are hereby advised that the next violation of this or any other work rule will result in a five-day suspension without pay. Continued violations of this type will lead to more serious disciplinary action, including termination.

It is my hope that this matter can be successfully remedied in the near future. Should you have any questions, or wish to discuss this in more detail, please notify me.

Sincerely,

B Brown

Supervisor Brown

cc: Union Steward
Personnel File

Discipline Case - Exhibit 2

VI

ARBITRATION OF GRIEVANCES

The process of arbitration is rooted deeply in history. Indeed, kings and other rulers such as Solomon have been deciding disputes throughout the centuries. In the last two- to three-hundred years, commercial arbitration has been utilized to obtain speedy and equitable decisions and avoid the hassles of the courts.

The concept of arbitration in the labor-management arena is a fairly recent development in the United States. Today it is such an accepted practice (94% of all negotiated agreements contain such a clause)[1] that the novelty of its application to labor relation is not generally appreciated.

Arbitration can be defined as a "simple preceeding voluntarily chosen by parties who want a dispute determined by an impartial judge of their own mutual selection, whose decision, based on the merits of the case, they can agree in advance to accept as final and binding."[2] It is a quasi-judicial process: "judicial" in the sense that it is enforceable in the courts and "quasi" in the sense that legal rules of evidence and interpretation are not strictly utilized.

Those who serve as arbitrators may be called by any of the following names: referee, umpire, neutral, impartial chairperson or (most commonly) arbitrator. They all mean the same thing: a professionally competent individual chosen by labor and management to render a decision on a dispute brought before him/her.

Unless specifically empowered by the collective bargaining agreement to do otherwise, the arbitrator is bound to reach a decision based upon the information supplied by the parties at the hearing before him/her and in post hearing briefs if they are desired by the parties. The arbitrator is an expert with agreements and arguments. He/She cannot be bluffed or fooled. A factual presentation of sound arguments, logically developed is what the arbitrator seeks to obtain from the parties so that an equitable decision based upon the agreement can be speedily rendered.

An arbitration hearing is a time when the parties to a dispute appear before the arbitrator to define the issue, present initial arguments, develop the facts of the case through the direct and cross-examination of witnesses and presentation of exhibits and summarize their case as a result of what has unfolded during the hearing itself. Hearings may be formal or informal, with most inclining toward the latter. A hearing may be a situation where there is no dispute as to the facts and is simply an attempt by each party to persuade the arbitrator that their interpretation of the agreement was the actual intent of the parties. In the other major category, or discharge cases, the facts are in dispute and each side will try to get the arbitrator to accept their perception of reality. Decisions in such cases almost invariably revolve around a question of credibility.

Arbitration also offers the parties another vital service. A hearing is the collective bargaining process on review. Conduct in the hearing may alter or reinforce the future relationships and behavior of the parties. It also enables the union to demonstrate to its membership how competently they can be represented as well as provide them with their "day in court" on the merits of their case. To the individual union member or manager, arbitration is frequently a source of rumor and mystique. A hearing will help dampen the rumor but usually enhances the mystique.

This section contains some specific information as to procedures for arbitration, the wisdom of going to arbitration and the guides which arbitrators apply in order to reach their decisions.

16.

UNDERSTANDING ARBITRATION

THOMAS E. CARLYLE

The unique character of the arbitration hearing, as a product of the style and discretion of the individual arbitrator, is probably the most widely accepted yet most indefinable dimension of the arbitration process. The parameters within which the arbitrator functions have their origin not so much in law as in professionally-established standards, such as those outlined in the "Code of Professional Responsibility for Arbitrators of Labor Management Disputes of the National Academy of Arbitrators, American Arbitration Association, and Federal Mediation and Conciliation Service."

The arbitration hearing is intended to provide a forum for the efficient, fair, and orderly presentation of their respective positions by the parties to a dispute. As a rule, the proceedings are less formal and more loosely structured than those associated with questions of law. Still, many of the constructs related to the operation of an arbitration hearing, such as burden of proof, admissibility and inadmissibility of evidence, and the procedural format, are derived from legal concepts.

There are, however, some elements of the arbitration hearing which are generally common denominators, regardless of how individual the proceedings may be. These would include: establishment of the issue or issues in dispute; submission of evidential exhibits; opening statements by the parties; direct and cross examination of witnesses, and summations.

After the proper correspondence has passed between the parties, establishing the intention to proceed to arbitration, the problem of determining the issue or issues to be placed before the arbitrator remains. Typically, this question is answered prior to the parties' arrival at the hearing, although it is possible that they may solicit the assistance of the arbitrator in making this determination.

A fundamental piece of evidence, and almost invariably the first jointly submitted, is the collective bargaining agreement. The agreement will usually contain a provision which defines the scope of the arbitrator's authority. In addition, the specific provisions related to the alleged violation are cited. Other documents which pertain to the grievance may also be submitted at this time.

Once agreement on what violation or violations are at issue has been reached, each party will be given an opportunity to make an opening statement. The intention here is to provide the arbitrator with a capulized picture of the dispute and familiarize him/her with the parties and the contractual language involved.

In keeping with the practice followed in the courtroom, the "moving party" will present its case first.

> Thus, in most cases involving contract interpretation, the union goes first since it is the moving party attempting to change the status quo. In cases involving challenges to discipline, the employer usually goes forward with the case, on the theory "that the employer took the precipitating action of imposing the discipline."[1]

The traditional order of presentation is as follows: an opening statement is offered by the moving party, after which the second party makes its opening statement; the first party will then present its evidence, cross-examination of its witnesses will be permitted, and rebuttals follow. The second party will then present its evidence, with cross-examination and rebuttals following. The party that opens will usually be the last to close.

Unless there is an exchange of briefs, the case closes at this point; otherwise, receipt by the arbitrator of the parties' briefs marks the case's closing. American Arbitration Association (AAA) guidelines suggest that the decision be handed down within thirty days; in practice, however, many arbitrators--especially those with exceedingly heavy caseloads--find that period of time somewhat confining.

Where permanent arbitrators are used, as, for example, in the coal industry, arbitration proceedings are generally more informal. Hearings tend to become more formal where an _ad hoc_ arbitrator is used, and especially where the issue to be decided is a highly emotional one or involves complicated questions of interpretation or application.

Arbitrators may, by state law, be given certain special quasi-legal powers, such as the authority to swear witnesses; over half of the states give arbitrators the power to issue subpoenas to compel the appearance of witnesses or the production of relevant documents.

Rules of evidence, strictly adhered to in courts of law, have a rather relaxed application in arbitration proceedings. As with other arbitration concepts which have their origin in law, they serve more as guidelines than gospel. The arbitrator's willingness to accept virtually any evidence which the parties wish to submit is based primarily on two assumptions: first, that the arbitrator, in the interests of justice, would do better to accept all evidence submitted, even though it may include the irrelevant, since it can later be screened out, than refuse some evidence and run the risk of excluding the relevant from consideration; secondly, that the arbitrator, as an experienced and learned practitioner in his/her profession, need not be afforded the same safeguards and protections that inexperienced lay jurists would need in the unfamiliar surroundings of the courtroom.

The laxness of the rules of evidence applies as well to questions of materiality, admissibility, relevance and, of special notability, to hearsay testimony. In a court of law, testimony based on a person's knowledge of matters told to him/her by another, and not on personal experience is not admissible. This principle is not stringently enforced in arbitration hearings, for the reasons outlined above, relating to a presumption of the arbitrator's ability as a professional to distinguish the relevant from the irrelevant, and credible testimony from incredible testimony.

As was discussed previously, the arbitrator's request for evidence is generally compelling. There are, however, some exceptions to this tenet. Privileged communications, as between a doctor and patient, an attorney and client, and a wife and husband, are exempted. A witness may also invoke the constitutional privilege to refuse to disclose information that would lead to self-incrimination with regard to a criminal act or omission. A witness who has legal access to classified government information likewise need not divulge it in the absence of government clearance permitting the arbitrator to examine such evidence.

Also in contrast to courtroom standards, during direct and cross-examination, leading questions on non-controversial subjects (job title, date of hire, etc.) may be permitted. This serves to expedite the hearing; again, the issue of the parameters of propriety are left to the discretion of the arbitrator. That is, improper questioning is not an impossibility. Questions may be deemed inappropriate if: (1) there is no discernible relationship between the question and the issue at hand; (2) the witness could not reasonably be expected to have knowledge of matters about which he or she is being asked; (3) the questioning takes on an intimidating or abusive nature; (4) the questioning deals with areas which have already been sufficiently covered; and (5) the questions are overly complex and involved. In this vein, a witness for one side should not be called for direct examination by the opposing party except under extraordinary circumstances.

The credibility of witnesses is a critical point on which many decisions turn. This is particularly true where the facts of the case are in dispute. Among the criteria frequently used to evaluate the credibility of witnesses are: the demeanor and manner of the witness; the character of the testimony; the witness' capacity to recollect, perceive, and communicate, the apparent honesty and veracity of the witness; the presence of a bias; and inconsistencies in the testimony.

The degree of proof required--"preponderance of evidence," "clear and convincing proof," or "proof beyond a reasonable doubt"--will depend primarily on the arbitrator's assessment of the seriousness of the charge. Generally, the more serious the charge, the greater the degree of proof required.

Although arbitration is an adversarial proceeding, it is important to keep in mind its purpose: dispute settlement. It is a method voluntarily chosen by the parties to settle disputes by presenting them to impartial judges selected by the parties themselves. Its purpose is the efficient settlement of disagreements, toward the ultimate goal of maintenance of stability in the labor/management relationship. The arbitration process is tied directly to collective bargaining and has been most successful where collective bargaining has been most successful.

FOOTNOTE

[1]Martin F. Schneinman, _Evidence and Proof in Arbitration_, (New York State School of Industrial Relations, 1977), p. 2, quoting Arnold Zack, _Understanding Grievance Arbtiration in the Public Sector_, report submitted to Division of Public

Employee Labor Relations, Office of Labor-Management Relations Services (Washington, DC: US Department of Labor, 1974), p. 24.

17.

ARBITRATION: UPDATING A VITAL PROCESS

JOHN ZALUSKY

The traditional labor arbitration procedure has grown in complexity until today it is taking on the appearance of a courtroom procedure. The presence of lawyers, use of transcripts, swearing in of witnesses, pre- and post-hearing briefs, and long delays throughout--in setting hearing dates, extending deadlines for the filing of briefs and waiting for the decision--are all too common. The arbitration process is so large and cumbersome it is beginning to discourage industrial justice for two very basic reasons: cost and delay.

Arbitration has a long history in our concept of justice. But its application to labor disputes--as the last step in the grievance procedure used to interpret or enforce a collective bargaining contract--is rather new. In its earliest use, Old English law books make reference to agreements to arbitrate commercial disputes in 1224, with arbitration viewed as a means to avoid the delays and costs of the legal system of the English courts.

In labor relations, arbitration was adopted, like its commercial predecessor, to avoid the alternative of going through the slow, complex, and costly court system, as well as the costly alternative of the strike. It is ironic then that cost and delay, two judicial characteristics arbitration was used to avoid, are now plaguing the arbitration process itself as it becomes more like a court procedure. More than 90 percent of major U.S. labor agreements have grievance arbitration provisions.

To endure, arbitration must be voluntary or freely agreed to. Yet once the parties agree to arbitrate, they agree to abide by the award; that is, the award is "final and binding" on both parties. Thus, it might be said that entry into the agreement is a free act, while abiding by the decision and award is "compulsory." The voluntary aspect is essential in a free society. Without this essential point workers do not have the option of fashioning an agreement to meet their needs and lack the right to strike. The right to strike is one of the ways a free society like ours is clearly differentiated from totaliarianism.

Over the years labor has supported voluntary alternatives to the strike. National unions have opted for the grievance-arbitration procedure in lieu of the strike in most cases--as those involving the immediate safety of workers on the job--but the strike can also be a costly, unjust and perilous solution to contract grievances.

However, there is a general dissatisfaction with traditional grievance arbitration as we know it today. Consequently, the AFL-CIO Executive Council has urged affiliated unions to bargain expedited arbitration procedures into their contracts. Many of today's problems with traditional arbitration stem from court decisions and public policy outside the relationship of labor and management.

Arbitration was the topic of three 1960 decisions by the Supreme Court which came to be known as the Steelworkers' trilogy. They strongly supported the arbitration concept, but have had the side effect of complicating the process. The court clearly defined arbitration and cut down the areas in which courts could function. The issue of arbitrability, or whether the award "draws its essence" from the agreement was established as the essential limit of court review. The intent was to strengthen the position of arbitration. However, the result has been that the issue of arbitrability is raised almost automatically by the opposing party as a means of keeping the avenue of appeals open. Consequently, transcripts began to be taken far more than necessary.

In 1974, in Alexander v. Gardner-Denver, the U.S. Supreme Court ruled that an arbitration resolution to a civil rights discrimination grievance does not prevent the aggrieved worker from bringing up the same issue through the provisions of the Civil Rights Act. This decision is bound to have an effect on the arbitration process. The parties and the arbitrator probably will find it necessary to add even more procedural formalities so that the entire proceedings can stand judicial review in court.

Thus, to some extent, the modern-day problems with arbitration go beyond the activities of labor, management and their jointly selected third-party arbitrators. Much of the delay, formality, and cost of arbitration can be attributed to public policy, the courts and the intervention of public law into the collective bargaining relationship. But there are cost and delay problems internal to the relationship between the parties.

How costly is arbitration? The Federal Mediation and Conciliation Service (FMCS) found the average cost of arbitrators' fees and expenses in 1975 was $621.31. Normally, the cost of the arbitrator is at most only 15 to 20 percent of the union's total cost in arbitration cases.

Costs to a local and international union include many other expenses. Among them is the cost of a transcript, sometimes taken at the request of the arbitrator. In 1976, a representative transcript price was $2.75 per page with 10-day delivery. If earlier delivery is desired, the price can go as high as $4 per page. Even an uncomplicated case develops 35 pages of transcript per hour, or just less than 200 pages per day. The reporter's day is six hours, with a minimum charge of $50 per day, and expenses are charged in some cases.

The higher cost is usually that of a lawyer, who charges at least $40 per hour for research time and $55 per hour when the time is spent interviewing witnesses, presenting a case or writing briefs. Thus legal fees on the simplest case can run over $1,000. Some unions use lawyers on the international or regional office payroll, and others use highly trained representatives, who consult lawyers but call them in to handle only exceptional cases. However it is done, expert advice costs money, either directly or indirectly, and it must be counted as an arbitration expense.

Lost time payments to witnesses and local union officers in the preparation and presentation of a case also cost. With average wages over $5 per hour, the grievant, two witnesses, and two union officers would easily exceed $200 per day of hearing.

Thus in the context of the total cost to a union, that arbitrator's fee of $621.31 in 1975, split by the parties, isn't the only place where cost-benefit improvements can be made. One estimate puts the total cost to the union in a simple case at $2,290, using average figures for all expenses.

Avoiding the formalized proceedings cuts the cost in terms of lawyers, transcripts, lost time, and probably union staff time. Furthermore, doing without briefs can cut the arbitrator's study time, which in 1975 averaged nearly two days.

Delay in obtaining an award from an arbitrator is frustrating to a union. A grievance-arbitration procedure is an essential service the union offers a worker--and when it takes a year or more, the union and workers feel justice has been denied.

The whole grievance process must also be looked at in terms of streamlining. This has been done with most of the expedited procedures and has helped with the resolution of delay problems in arbitration.

In 1975, the FMCS reported a time between grievance date to arbitrator's award was 223 days--

or 7 1/3 months--with 181 days needed before the hearing date and 42 days after. And these figures are only averages. In view of these figures, it is obvious that most of the delay stems from delays in the grievance procedure.

The grievance procedures in labor agreements vary widely in terms of the number of steps required and the time limits permitted the employer and union at each step. The most common number of grievance steps is three; yet, 25 percent of union contracts have a four-step procedure, and some have five.

Sixty-three percent of the grievance procedures require that the first-step grievance be presented in writing, and it is presumed that the remaining 37 percent permit oral presentation. Less than 60 percent of the collective bargaining agreements surveyed by the Bureau of National Affairs place time limits on management's first-step response. Those that do permit one day at the first step in 21 percent of the agreements, two days in 37 percent, three days in 20 percent, and finally five days in 8 percent. As the dispute moves up the grievance steps, the time limits for responses normally increase.

The prehearing phase provides an insight into the delays. The time between the filing of the grievance and the requesting of a panel of arbitrators averaged 68 days in 1975.

As a rule of thumb, efficiency is served when grievances are handled at the lowest possible level. But there are many cases a foreman obviously can't resolve, so the first step can be a waste of time. For example, a time study grievance might as well go directly to the industrial engineering department which as the authority to change the standard. The same is true when the personnel department discharges or suspends a worker for absenteeism--the first-step management person has no authority. A close look at corporate decision-making can help reduce the time in the grievance steps.

A different problem also related to the first steps of the grievance procedure occurs when front-line supervisors and stewards fail to use the authority they do have. One way of reducing this problem is contract language providing that early resolution of grievances does not create precedent. This reduces the pressure on these early participants in the process. Another way of achieving the same result is by keeping the grievance verbal as long as possible, often through the second step.

Other devices used to cut delays prior to arbitration require that stewards and committee members in the first steps prepare fact-finding reports or sheets jointly with their management counterparts. These reports describe the areas of agreement on facts, those areas where agreement could be reached and proposals offered to resolve the matter. Unions using this procedure say they find more girevances are resolved at the early states. The written material also helps the grievance or bargaining committee in the last steps of the procedure, when the decision must be made whether to recommend arbitration. Some agreements allow this record to be used in arbitration and others do not. Obviously, resolving grievances is a very individual matter, and must be tailored to fit each bargaining relationship.

In some local unions, the membership must

make the decision as to whether a grievance should be arbitrated. Regardless of the pros and cons on this method, it consumes times, particularly in the summer months when some locals suspend membership meetings.

After the decision to arbitrate, more time can be lost in trying to match schedules among the various union and management representatives, lawyers and arbitrators. The more people involved, and the busier they are, the more the delay.

Stipulating agreement to some facts and the issue before the hearing can save time--but can also waste time. Thus the effort should be abandoned if it produces no quick agreement, for the arbitrator will normally shape and describe the issue and seek agreement on the facts early in the hearing anyway.

Throughout the process, the parties should be allowed to explore each others' position and all the facts supporting their positions. Holding back information to use as surprise evidence serves no purpose except delay, since if either side is confronted with new facts, the arbitrator will probably adjourn the hearing to let them study the new evidence. So when the surprise is removed, all that's left is the delay. If both parties had been open, the new facts might have helped resolve the issue in the grievance procedure.

The FMCS has modified the use of its computer system, limiting it to the selection of arbitrators and not using it in their assignment of cases. But use of FMCS computers has cut the delay between request for a panel and the date it is assigned from 16 days in 1973 to seven days in 1976. This time period can be improved if the parties keep a supply of request forms on hand and provide all the required information when making a request for a panel of arbitrators to either the FMCS or the American Arbitration Association (AAA).

Real improvements have been made across the board--in formality, cost and delay--through expedited arbitration.

The Steelworkers negotiated the pattern-setting expedited arbitration procedure in 1971 with the major steel companies. Their program developed from an intensive study of the overburdened traditional arbitration system and the joint labor-management committee's report solved real problems with the grievance procedure as well as with traditional arbitration.

The grievance procedure was redesigned to encourage resolution of grievances at the first two steps of the procedure. These two steps are oral and do not prejudice the position of either party. The participation of the worker and the foreman are required in step two to insure a disclosure of all facts. After the step two hearing, a written record records all facts that are agreed to, the facts in dispute, and the issue as seen by the parties. Step three is the channeling step. Here the grievance is reviewed and resolved, if possible, by labor and management. If it is not resolved it is referred to expedited arbitration if it is non-precedent setting, or to step four for complex issues or those likely to set precedent. Step four is a part of the traditional procedure and involves an earnest effort to resolve non-routine grievances based on the record developed between step two and three by top union and management officials.

The arbitrators used in the Steelworkers' program of expedited arbitration are drawn from strategically located geographical panels. The arbitrator to be used in a particular case is determined by rotation on that panel and avialability to hear that case within the prescribed time limits.

The expedited cases are referred directly from step three of the grievance procedure back to the local parties for expedited arbitration, subject to the approval of the national union's representative and the corporate counterpart. If either objects to the use of the expedited procedure, the case is referred to step four and potentially on to the traditional procedure. Most cases referred back to the local for expedited handling are resolved short of arbitration.

Appeal must be made within 10 days after the minutes of the step are received by the local parties. The parties then schedule a hearing date within 10 days of the appeal and the arbitrator is expected to make a decision within 48 hours.

The hearings are informal with no briefs filed or transcripts made. The rules of evidence are informal with the arbitrator obligated to insure a full and fair hearing.

Lawyers are not used by either side, but this is by understanding and is not a part of the formal agreement.

The arbitrator may refer complex or novel grievances back to the fourth step of the grievance procedure. The parties may mutually agree to refer a case back to the fourth step for the same reason.

The decisions of arbitrators in this procedure may not be used by the parties as a precedent in other cases.

Although this procedure was adopted by both parties in 1971 as experimental, it continues to be used nearly six years later to the satisfaction of both the companies and the union. There is still concern over the number of grievances that are not resolved early in the grievance procedure and are moved to arbitration. More than half of the cases approved for expedited arbitration are resolved by the local parties.

The Steelworkers are able to negotiate, implement and administer this system in large part because they negotiate on a national basis with the steel industry. However, it has now been expanded to other industries. With some differences in the expedited procedures used, the concept applied in basic steel is now used in the Alcoa, Reynolds Metals, National Can, Libby McNiell & Libby, Kennecott Copper and other Steelworker agreements.

Experience with 2,700 cases shows this system has cut the average cost of a case per party to the area of $55 and the awards are almost always given within the time limits.

When considering the quality of justice, the union finds little difference in the results between the expedited procedure and the traditional procedure. One grievance committee chairman is quoted as describing the performance of the expedited arbitrator "as being on a par with the members of the U.S. Steel Board of Arbitration," which is the chief tribunal of their traditional procedure.

In 1973, the U.S. Postal Service entered into an expedited arbitration agreement with the Postal Workers, the Letter Carriers, Mail Handlers and Laborers. The Postal Service had recently made the transition to free collective bargaining and the unions had to anticipate the diverse problems of grievances as different as a rural post office is from New York City. Furthermore, four national unions under one agreement had to be assured of consistent interpretations of the agreement.

The result was essentially three different arbitration procedures. Grievances over contract interpretations and disciplinary actions involving removal of a worker from the job went to two different traditional arbitration procedures.

The more formal traditional procedure has become overburdened. In June 1976, the contract that expired 11 months before still had 2,300 grievances pending arbitration. All together, 13,359 cases had been filed under this 1973-75 agreement. After less than a year under the new 1975-78 agreement, 8,000 grievances had been filed.

The expedited arbitration procedure is working much better than these two traditional procedures, but not as well as expected. The parties are now moving some of the backlog from the traditional to the expedited procedure by mutual agreement; and improvements, in the much smaller backlog of expedited cases, are expected. So in this case expedited arbitration offers a chance to save a system that was becoming overwhelmed without it.

Expedited or nonremoval discipline cases leave the grievance procedure at what amounts to the third step. The expedited procedure uses regional panels with arbitrators appointed by the AAA and the FMCS on a rotation basis, depending on geographic area. Both FMCS and AAA serve as the administrators. When AAA is the administrator, a $100 filing fee per case is shared by the parties. The arbitrators' usual fees tend to be about $200 per case, also shared equally.

The arbitrators are expected to hear the case within 10 days of notice. However, because of the backlog, delays have been much longer. In June 1976, 223 of these cases were pending arbitration. Once the case is heard, the arbitrator is expected to give a bench award with a written opinion within 48 hours. No briefs or transcripts are used, and awards do not set precedent. Although use of lawyers is not prohibited, neither side has used them as a matter of practice.

The unions exercise control over the process by channeling fourth step grievances through its arbitration board. Grievances are channeled by the board to expedited arbitration, national arbitration, or back to the local. In cases sent back, the local can arbitrate the matter if it chooses, but at its own expense. The arbitration board essentially gives the union the ability to oversee the process and channel issues to proper forums.

Generally, Postal Worker officials believe the expedited procedure has worked well for a new collective bargaining situation, and that the quality of justice has not been sacrificed to speed. However, the enormous number of grievances and the resulting backlog of arbitration cases remain a major problem.

Under the Mine Workers' expedited procedure, all grievances going to arbitration go to the expedited procedure but then may be appealed to an arbitration review board made up of one industry representative, one union representative and an impartial umpire. Appeals must be based on a claim that the initial arbitrator's decision conflicts with other awards on contract interpretation, other awards by the arbitration review board, or that the award was arbitrary, capricious or fraudulent. Another unique feature is that the district arbitrator may rule based on the record of the final grievance step meeting without actually holding a formal hearing. However, in cases involving issues of fact, hearings are generally held.

The Mine Workers' procedure permits the parties to carefully review arbitrator awards for consistency and conflict with federal law. However, at the Mine Workers 1976 convention, the membership demanded restoration of the right to strike during the next negotiations.

The right to strike on grievances has a long history in mining labor relations. Recent membership dissatisfaction has been fed by employers' refusal to implement expedited awards until all appeals to the review board have been exhausted. Since the review board had a big backlog of cases, inordinate time was lost without the right to strike between the negotiation of this system and its actual implementation.

The AFL-CIO Industrial Union Department has been instrumental in developing the Columbus, Ohio, Mini-Arbitration Program. This program is community based rather than industry or company based, and open to use by any interested union and employer in the Columbus area. In mini-arbitration, the FMCS assists the parties by designating an arbitrator for the specific case from a pre-selected roster.

Under these procedural rules the parties select a date and the FMCS then obtains from the roster an arbitrator able to hear the case on that date. The arbitrators' fees are on a scale of time and cases heard--$100 per half day for one or two cases, $150 per full day for one of two cases, and $200 per full day for three or four cases. Decisions are to be mailed to the parties within 48 hours after the close of the hearing.

The Columbus mini-arbitration system differs from other expedited procedures in that it spells out the offer of a service to both company and union with arbitrators ready to serve. Many aspects are left to the parties, such as whether or not the parties will use lawyers, transcripts, or briefs.

The developers of the Columbus Mini-Arbitration are now in the process of encouraging unions and employers in the region to bargain its service into their agreements. Since its implementation will await contract expiration dates, or parties adopting the program on a case-by-case basis, it will be some time before enough case experience is available to assess mini-arbitration. However, it is well designed, supported by labor and management, and has every prospect of achieving its goals.

Under an Allied Industrial Workers' agreement in Meadville, PA, issues move to the accelerated procedure by mutual agreement and neither lawyers, transcripts nor briefs are used. Awards are due within 48 hours after the hearing, which must be scheduled within 10 days of appeal.

A panel of seven arbitrators was selected by the parties from an FMCS list of arbitrators in the geographic area. The FMCS agreed to act as secretary for the panel by choosing from the pre-selected panel an arbitrator able to hear the case within the time limits.

This system has been in effect for over a year and has never had a single case. Yet it was negotiated, in part, because of a backlog of cases. Cases have not only been resolved short of arbitration, the grievance procedure is now working effectively.

Unions without national agreements also have many problems with costs and delay. But many local unions have made real progress by embodying the essentials of the expedited procedures in their contracts or by simply negotiating the AAA's expedited rules into their agreements.

From the employer's point of view, the advantages are often the nonprecedent setting aspect of the quick award and the reduction of potentially large backpay obligations. The union, of course, gains reduced costs and delays and it has usually been achieved without a loss in the quality of justice.

The AAA offers a special set of expedited rules that a union and company can either negotiate into their agreement or use on a case-by-case basis.

The AAA's expedited rules provide that the regional office of the AAA appoint an available arbitrator and fix the time and place for the hearing. No transcript is used and the award is made within five days of the hearing. The AAA charges a $100 service fee per case. The arbitrators' fees and expenses are separate from the service fee. Other provisions, such as limits on lawyers, tighter time limits, or a ban on setting precedent can be added by the parties. When adopting to AAA's rules, local unions should specify the publication date of the rules to protect against being forced to adopt automatically all changes initiated by the AAA.

Well-known, established arbitrators on the AAA's panel have agreed to arbitrate under these rules so the procedure is ready to operate as soon as it is agreed to. In fact, a local and company may try the procedure during the term of an existing agreement simply by jointly notifying AAA that the company and union have agreed to move selected cases to this procedure.

Notable examples of agreements using this procedure are a Paperworkers' agreement with International Paper and a United Transportation Union agreement with Long Island Railroad.

Thus the overall experience of expedited arbitration after about five years is that it is widely accepted and is achieving its goals of reducing both cost and delay throughout the process. There is no evidence that the quality of justice has suffered, with union representatives usually reporting there is no difference.

The variety of programs available indicates that the concept is adaptable. The AAA and FMCS are willing to assist within their limits and some parties have worked out their own systems.

In short, expedited arbitration is used and does work in almost all conceivable settings.

However, it's essential that the whole grievance arbitration process must be streamlined, not just the arbitration step. The greatest share of time normally lost occurs before the arbitration hearing--so reform must be viewed in the whole context.

Reprinted with permission, American Federationist, John Zalusky, November, 1976. pp. 1-8.

ABOUT THE CONTRIBUTORS

THOMAS E. CARLYLE - is currently a Research Assistant, Department of Labor Relations, Indiana University of Pennsylvania.

ROBERT L. GAYLOR - is currently Director of Employee Relations and Special Assistant to the President, Indiana University of Pennsylvania.

KATHRYN HOFFNER - is currently Coordinator of Student Development and Assistant Director of Financial Aid, Bowling Green State University, Ohio.

PAUL E. HOFFNER - is currently Professor and Staff Associate, Center for the Study of Labor Relations, Indiana University of Pennsylvania.

KEVIN JORDAN - is currently a Research Assistant, Department of Labor Relations, Indiana University of Pennsylvania.

KENNETH A. KOVACH - is currently Professor of Business Administration, George Mason University, Virginia.

DONALD S. MCPHERSON - is currently Professor and Staff Associate, Center for the Study of Labor Relations, Indiana University of Pennsylvania.

FREDERICK H. NESBITT - is currently Professor and Staff Associate, Center for the Study of Labor Relations, Indiana University of Pennsylvania.

KATHLEEN A. ROHALY - is currently a Research Assistant, Department of Labor Relations, Indiana University of Pennsylvania.

DAVID C. WARHOLIC - is currently Professor of Business Management, Shippensburg State College, Pennsylvania.

JOHN ZULASKY - is currently a Research Associate on the national staff of the AFL-CIO.

ABOUT THE EDITORS

PAUL E. HOFFNER - is currently a Professor of Labor Relations and Staff Associate, Center for the Study of Labor Relations, Indiana University of Pennsylvania. Professor Hoffner, formerly a faculty member at Mankato State University (MN), and a Labor Relations Specialist with the Commonwealth of Pennsylvania Department of Education, is engaged in both consulting and writing in the field of labor-management relations and compensation administration.

ROBERT L. GAYLOR - is currently Executive Assistant to the President and Director of Employe Relations, Indiana University of Pennsylvania. Mr. Gaylor previously served as Director of Labor Relations for the Commonwealth of Pennsylvania Department of Education and has also taught courses in labor-management relations for Pepperdine University. In addition, Mr. Gaylor serves on a variety of Labor-Management organizations and is a frequent participant at seminars on labor relations in higher education.

KATHLEEN A. ROHALY - is currently a Research Assistant, Department of Labor Relations, Indiana University of Pennsylvania.